NOT IN FRONT
OF THE TELLY

75 Years of the BBC's
Complaints Department

Ed Harris

Illustrations by David Lock

Polperro Heritage Press

First published in Great Britain by the Polperro Heritage Press

ISBN 0-9530012-5-3

Published by
Polperro Heritage Press
Clifton-upon-Teme
Worcestershire WR6 6EN

Printed by Orphans Press
Leominster HR6 8JT

CONTENTS

PROLOGUE

Inevitably it was raining. On and off. As it tends to do a lot in Belfast. Otherwise it was a bright if a little blustery morning in the May of 1999. A military helicopter hovered back and forth across the small square of sky framed between the rooftops. Assembled in a pleasantly planted atrium of the otherwise architecturally indifferent BBC Northern Ireland's Blackstaff House was some of the BBC's great and good. Joining them were executives and staff of Capita, a specialist customer services provider to the public sector. Together with special guest Mo Mowlam, the (then) Secretary of State for Northern Ireland, and other dignitaries, the scene was set for the official opening of the BBC's first purpose-built Information Centre.

The Chairman of the BBC, Sir Christopher Bland, noted in his speech that it was 75 years ago almost to the day that the fledgling British Broadcasting Company created its first dedicated interface with its radio audience. Since then, in excess of some thirty-seven and a half million viewers and listeners had either written or telephoned to comment or complain, with probably just as many wondering why. But now the time had come for the BBC to hand over this part of the operation to the experts so that it could concentrate on its core remit of making and broadcasting programmes.

Mercifully, neither the Minister, the Chairman nor any of the great and the good had a go at answering calls from members of the public, which was a wise move. On a previous occasion, when senior managers were being encouraged to do a stint on the telephones, a particularly difficult caller was unimpressed with the answers he was receiving and demanded to be put through to the top man. Perhaps unwisely, he was informed that he was indeed through to the Managing Director. Upon which the call terminated with a clear and unequivocal: 'Oh, yeah? And I'm Donald fucking Duck!!!'

INTRODUCTION

Love it or hate it, the British Broadcasting Corporation holds a particular fascination. Of that there is no doubt. Column metres continue to fill up tabloids and broadsheets alike with Auntie's antics. Millions of people watch or listen to some BBC every week. And just as many telephone it, write to it, email it, surf it on the Internet or talk about it in the pub, on the bus, or to themselves. The history of the BBC has been documented well enough. What it is and what it stands for has for decades flowed forth tirelessly and worthily. The same, however, cannot be said for what might be described as the public's domain - those bits of the BBC where ordinary people go to complain, comment or criticize. And this is their story.

As I sit here pounding out my pontifications about the BBC, I am acutely aware that many others will be doing likewise by letter, telephone or email. When I first arrived on this curious scene in the late 1970s, the BBC had legions of staff dutifully devoted to the practice of addressing the often weird and wonderful concerns of its audiences. The word 'accountability' however, had not by then truly entered the BBC lexicon as an active verb. Despite the fact that she had traditionally taken a lot of stick for most of her life, Auntie actually did very little to defend herself. Worse than forever rolling over and just taking it, she promoted the general perception of a distant, indifferent, somewhat superior creature verging on the arrogant. The end of the seventies saw out the last 'Old Labour' government and ushered in the arrival of the Thatcher era. These were the twilight years of 'Old Britain' with its strikes, its demarcation lines and restrictive practices. The country was thirsting for a change, which it got by the bucket load. And the good ship BBC was to be by no means exempt.

The BBC lumbered into the 1980s fully loaded with a crew imbued with the last gleaming of a founding principle that Auntie knew best. Few appeared to have a clue let alone the slightest concern about the storm that was brewing; a storm that served to decimate even the highest and the mightiest and which has continued unabated ever since. It could be that I was more used to change than many others around me at that time. Before I arrived at the BBC, I had experienced the last vestiges of Victorian splendour at Lloyd's of London. I had tasted the last years of Granada Television under the auspices of its founding Bernstein brothers. As an actor/stage manager, I took the final curtain of Weekly Rep' and Summer Season. At the National Theatre and in the film industry, there was a sense that the days of the closed shop were numbered. I remember feeling that at the BBC I was again on the cusp of fundamental change. And was I right, or was I right?

With the twinkle of a first child on the way and an ongoing commitment to something called a mortgage, the time had arrived to settle and, for the first time in eleven years, hold down a 'proper job'. My semi-bohemian lifestyle was over. The decision made, I duly reported to what was known as a Job Shop wherein lost souls such as I underwent a series of tests geared to result in a career match. I was required to disclose all of my work experience and interests, which were many and varied to say the least. Suffice to say that my test results were not easily translatable. There were few opportunities available for an actor-manager-playwright-would-be-impresario who could cut film as deftly as build and strike a West End stage set. The wheel of fortune finally arrived at a choice between a gravedigger in the local cemetery and a six-month contract in the BBC Filmstores. My core aspiration to become a novelist favoured the former, but the threat of divorce secured the latter.

To say the least, arriving at the BBC was a bit of a culture shock. To find actors, musicians and stage crews on pensionable contracts, with weekends off, paid holidays and sick pay. And all the terminology. I was instructed to 'report' to an entity known as the 'AaiC' which, in regular language, meant the Acting Assistant in Charge. To my horror the BBC was more like another branch of the Civil Service; a vast lumbering bureaucracy fuelled by copious amounts of memos, forms and paperclips, punctuated with mind-numbing terminology such as BoG and BoM, Secretariat and Registry; comprising

9

numerous Directorates dotted with endless designations such as HOB&E (Tel), CAProgIf, HPresTel, and, even (truly): EIEIO. This, so the story goes, was the Executive Instructor Engineering Information Office. One holder of that post was said to have been an Oliver MacDonald, who took great delight in signing his memos - O MacDonald, EIEIO.

Closer to this account, there was the dubious designation of DOM, which stood for Duty Office Manager. Kept in a drawer was a 'duty tie' to be used for special occasions. At first glance it was a very nice tie. But on closer inspection it revealed the repeat pattern of a naked old man displaying his wares from within an open raincoat. Thus the corruption of DOM can be left to the imagination. Another (rather sad) manager used to revel in the delights of his various designations. He would always answer the phone with his latest acronym as he progressed through the corporation. When he decided to merge Home and Foreign Traffic Units, he was narrowly dissuaded from choosing Central Unit News Traffic.

*

I also discovered that BBC people didn't take holidays or vacations, but 'Authorised Absences', or 'Leave'. There was in fact a small family of 'Leave Applications', such as: Sick, Annual, Compassionate, Maternal, Unpaid and Short Notice. The latter once comprised two days known as 'bisques'. Quite what 'bisque' meant I never did find out. Whatever, they were 'awarded' if, God forbid, the washing machine died and you had to wait in for a man to come and fix it. So it was with all these treasures, as well as a regular monthly wage, that was sufficient to restrain my inherent wanderlust. On expiration of my six-month temporary contract, I became a permanent member of BBC staff. Eager to make my way if not my mark, I set my sights on getting as quickly as possible to what I perceived to be the epicentre of the operation, Television Centre. I was familiar with Broadcasting House from my days as a member of *The Radio One Club*, but that was about it.

Adventures In The Complaints Trade

FIRST IMPRESSIONS

It all really started for me when I happened upon a vacancy for an Assistant in something called the Television Duty Office. The job description called for a thorough knowledge of the BBC and its programmes, a good telephone manner and a sense of humour. Devoid of or untested in all but the last of these attributes, I rang up and spoke to an affable lady who at that time was the manager and made an appointment to see her. The Television Duty Office, situated on the fourth floor of Television Centre, blissfully yards from the BBC Club, was a tiny room comprising a huddle of three desks forming a square in the centre. A long table sat against the inner wall upon which were placed two typewriters and above them a huge bulk of green card index boxes. A collection of beautifully bound copies of *Radio Times* going back decades shared half of another wall. Metal cabinets containing a modest collection of reference books and assorted files occupied the other half. Another desk sat apart from the rest by the window, opposite a pair of television sets: one tuned to BBC-1 and the other to BBC-2.

One of the five telephones was held close to the bowed head of an unhappy looking young man, intoning a series of acknowledgement murmurs. Another instrument sat ringing before a jolly looking woman tapping a long length of ash into a brown Bakelite ashtray. She smiled and asked in a low, husky voice if I was Ed. On confirmation, the remains of her cigarette indicated for me to take the seat opposite her, which I did. As she went on to politely greet her call, so the young man to my right concluded his with a heavy sigh of relief. For a few seconds he watched his instrument like a cat stalking potential prey. When it showed no further sign of life, he turned to me, smiled broadly and introduced himself.

Before the next call he managed to brief me about the Duty Office and what was required of those who manned it. There was the business of the licence fee to understand: where it went, on what and why it existed at all. The structure of the BBC: who did what, why, where and when; the thousands of programmes and as many presenters and stars, and all the issues arising, past and present. Then there was the history of the corporation, including more than a passing familiarity with the Royal Charter. There was the Press with whom one had to be careful not to have any contact and policy about which one was never to spout. It was lunchtime and I had arrived at the very coalface of BBC accountability.

Before I arrived at the BBC, I had not really given much thought to it. Like milk on the doorstep each morning, it had always been there. Only when I set up home for myself did I give any thought to the licence fee. It was simply yet another bill I was expected to pay and duly paid it (mostly). I thought as much about what it actually represented as I did the water rates or the gas bill, which wasn't a lot. But suddenly being placed at the end of a telephone and listening to often manic pronouncements about how people were 'forced' to pay a government levy for 'filth, depravity and rubbish' brought home to me a very different, if not disturbing, worldview.

To my mind, if I didn't like something then I wouldn't watch it. Simple as that. Sure, being a child of the television age, it was difficult to comprehend life without the box, but I was always able to distinguish between what I liked and what I did not. If I didn't like something then, like most people (or so I thought) I simply switched off, bitched about it to whoever was around at the time, or to myself. The thought of actually calling a television company to complain had never occurred to me. I really had no idea that this strange process existed, let alone that it had been going on for decades.

I quickly learned that life in the Television Duty Office was not just about the BBC but also about people. Trainee psychiatrists could find no better place to truly get to grips with the finer points of social (and anti-social) behaviour. Those moments, for example, familiar to anyone who has done the job when a glottal stop of monumental proportions earnestly and loudly demands: "GIVE ME THE DIRECTOR GENERAL!"

I well remember my first 'difficult' call.

Having survived the regular barrage of threats and promises of personal retribution, I managed to grab an opportunity to request some idea of what the problem was. The frenzied tones gave way to a quivering imitation of calm under great duress. I was told in no uncertain terms that I should have been watching the television screen: "AT TEA-TIME!!! DURING THE CHILDREN'S PROGRAMMES!! IN A CARTOON OF ALL THINGS!!!!!"

"'WHAT?!!!!" barked the distraught mother of three when I told her that we were not aware of anything particularly untoward.

"FILTH" boomed the response: "DISGUSTING FILTH."

I asked if she could be a little more specific.

"SPECIFIC!!???," she thundered. "YOU EXPECT ME TO REPEAT THAT FILTHY, DISGUSTING FILTH??!!!"

I didn't, of course and told her so, adding my great surprise that Yogi Bear or any of his cheeky chums could be guilty of such behaviour.

"IT WAS WHAT WAS EMBLAZONED ACROSS THE SCREEN FOR ALL THE WORLD TO SEE - FILTH! FOUL, DISGUSTING, FILTH!!"

Without further ado I took the caller's name and telephone number and promised to get back to her just as soon as the tape had been checked. In my mind's eye I could see the potential headline for the next day's tabloids: **Yogi's Bear-faced BBC Boo-Boo**

The next half-hour or so was an anxious time. I picked up one call after another. Requests for music details; transcripts of programmes; the 'back doctor' featured on *Tomorrow's World* seven years ago - or was it the bone specialist four years ago on Thames TV? And so on. Until the familiar strains of one that I was soon to recognise as 'a regular' enquired: "Hello darling, is Terry there?"

I groaned. 'Darling' was the generic greeting offered to whoever had the misfortune to answer. And 'Terry' was none other than the esteemed Wogan himself.

"I'm afraid he's not here," I replied truthfully.

"I'm in the cupboard", she whispered conspiratorially, "Sshh. Have to be quiet. Make a noise like a little bit of cheese."

She was (and remains I believe) an inoffensive soul - unlike some other 'regulars' and was known as the 'War Widow' because her pension was the only other topic apart from Terry Wogan that seemed to occupy her life. And in turn, ours. Why she called from the confines of her cupboard was never established. What was apparent however was that she needed someone to talk at. And that someone, at that particular moment, just happened to be me. Like many, the BBC was her friend, and those working in the Duty Office her special friends. Whether or not such indulgences constitute the best expenditure of the licence fee is debatable. But then those who ponder such things have invariably never been ear-to-ear with the effect a caring 'Auntie' can, and does, have on some of her more vulnerable nieces and nephews.

*

The matchstick inserted deep under my fingernail was close to drawing blood when the internal number flashed. It was my call. I mouthed to my colleague 'War Widow'. Born truly of close comradeship in the face of such shared experiences, we flicked the switches on each of our units to exchange calls. From the confines of her cupboard, the War Widow was unaware she was whispering her sweet nothings to someone completely different.

Duly armed with the necessary information, I rang back my distraught mother of three, allowing her to savage me for the amount of time it had taken, and accepting the threat that this too would be added to the growing list of grievances to be put to the Home Secretary. The sound of another cigarette being furiously lit allowed me to reveal the result of my enquiries. A word had indeed appeared on screen during the cartoon. Phonetically it could be taken as a swear word. In fact it was a famous Hollywood trade name. Bolex, I explained manufactured film cameras. And it was pronounced Bow-lex.

It was around this time that readers of the late lamented *Listener* magazine were plunged into our surreal world, the inhabitants of which were just as likely to be asked for details of how to make logs from damp newspapers as they were to fall prey to 'an inexplicable and anonymous stream of abuse'. The patience and long-suffering nature of Duty Office staff was applauded. As in the case of the elderly man who called every week in the (vain) hope of obtaining a cheap sexual thrill.

As regular as clockwork, every Thursday, he would call on the pretext of wanting to know what horse races were being transmitted the coming Saturday. Having been given that information he would pause before moving on to nonchalantly enquire who was going to be on *Top of the Pops* that evening. He would breathlessly acknowledge each name in turn before asking: "Are Zoo (the show's resident dance troupe at the time) going to be on tonight?" And if so, "what will they be wearing?" That information wasn't available and he was told as much every time. But he still continued to call, week in, week out.

Then there was the very grand 'Mrs H.' She would either arrive on the 'phone already in full flight or await her cue of "Duty Office, good evening." Whereupon she would issue a lengthy and meaningless monologue about her family's history and her relationship with the Royal Family. More than a few minutes of this would pass before she would break into song, then drop the 'phone to the floor with a loud crash. The finalé to this experience would be strains of a badly tuned piano resonating from across the far side of the room. The sight of a Tory Minister on the screen was sufficient provocation to trigger another 'regular' to give the BBC hell. He would rant and rave until the sound of a struggle would interrupt his flow. His voice would become less and less audible as he was carted away down a long, echoing corridor.

Then there was Mr P who claimed to have been employed as an actor by the BBC in the 1940s and was still awaiting his cheque. He would call regularly from the Salvation Army Hostel in Whitechapel where he 'currently lodged'. His opening line would always be: "Hello, P here, indubitably". He would then launch into his all-too-familiar tale of woe. He was a harmless old boy and was treated with great respect. So much so, the staff had a whip round one Christmas in lieu of his fee. He later reported his deep gratitude to the Duty Officer for 'assistance in this matter – indubitably'. However not all 'regulars' were held in such high regard. Take Commander M. He would ring up to have a go at staff whenever he felt like it. Having issued his quota of personal abuse he would add (gruffly) "Will you have a gin-and-tonic with me after work, sailor?"

The BBC Duty Officer had to have a finger on the pulse at all times. The weekly Programme Review meeting and advance copies of *Radio Times* would provide some useful pre-transmission information. But such is the nature of broadcasting that even the best intelligence is often absolutely no guarantee of success. A woman once called from the Conservative Party. She was having 15 or so lady friends around to her house that evening to watch *Dallas* and wanted to know if the episode of *Smiley's People* following would be just as suitable. There was no reason to suppose otherwise as this series had been a roaring success. There had been no problem with content before and there was no reason to suppose that this episode would be any exception. Except that it contained a raunchy nightclub scene, complete with half-naked men in black leather jock-straps. So much for 'that nice man' at the BBC.

'The Duty Office art is a delicate one', the *Listener* innocently observed, 'positioned as it was 'on the front line between the immovable object of the Corporation and the irresistible force of the enraged licence-holder.' It was not the job of the Duty Officer, readers were ill-informed, to express a personal opinion, but to offer the BBC view where possible. 'The Duty Officer plays a holding action and wins by not giving in. One slip and the caller may be on the phone all night, demanding access to someone higher up who went home hours ago.' Realistically this was a tough call for one or two workers at the coalface of accountability who were not immune from the odd slip or ten. In fact it would be many years before this genetic flaw was eradicated. Meanwhile, picking up the 'phone at one's convenience, answering the call and then putting the instrument down again was, for some, the closest it ever came to what we think of today as customer care. The idea of offering 'a positive experience' was a perception that would have been greeted with not a little incredulity by some old timers.

Up to the early eighties, the service provided by the Television Duty Office could at best be described as variable. It had in some respects traditionally taken its cue very much from the business of Television, which was altogether far brasher and much less interested in 'playing Auntie' than was its radio sibling. The pace and sheer weight of traffic generated by television did not always allow for the same degree of patience and understanding. In fairness, however, most staff enjoyed an excellent relationship with the vast majority of the thousands who telephoned or wrote each week; some less so.

A newspaper diarist once called the Television Duty Office expecting to be greeted by a 'civil servant type' who would thoughtfully log his complaint with a 'Thank you, Sir, have a nice weekend'. However the diarist was somewhat taken aback to find himself quickly embroiled in a blazing row 'conducted at high decibel level.' Even the threat of 'a thundering *Sunday Times* editorial' had no effect on the Duty Officer's behaviour who declared: "We're not interested in the *Sunday Times* here".

A concerted effort to legislate how the BBC related to those who funded it was a distant ambition. Which in all provided a secure habitation for those individuals who chose to take their cue from the popular perception of the BBC as arrogant and dismissive. There was the acquaintance of a journalist who was also a parent. He had rung the Television Duty Office to complain that a dancing sequence featured on the *Rock and Pop Awards* was, in his opinion, pornographic. Naturally enough, when he telephoned, he expected nothing less than a professional service from the BBC. Instead, the 'outraged parent' found himself writing to the journalist of his acquaintance to report: 'the duty officer conveyed perfectly that he despised my view'. Worse, while not denying that the dancing was pornographic, the duty officer then asked the precise nature of the complaint. Thus goaded, the outraged parent replied that in his view simulated sex was unnecessary and undesirable, particularly with children watching. "Ah", replied the duty officer smugly, "but the Rock and Pop Awards is not a children's programme".

It was of course irksome that such reports would find their way into the papers with wearisome regularity. But let's face it, such examples make for good copy. At the time some would (and did) argue that's how it is at the sharp end of any public service. Rules governing the behaviour of staff did exist, as did disciplinary procedures. But these were only as good as a management structure willing to exercise them, which was rare. Proper training provision for what has become a customer service industry simply did not exist. Training was something undertaken by programme makers and broadcasting professionals.

More than one troublesome member of staff had for too long inhabited that zone of exasperation known as 'the plateau of tolerance'. But one in particular most readily comes to mind. Courtesy once again of the *Listener* magazine again we can pay a visit the Far Side; the genie in the Duty Office bottle; the worst scenario just waiting to happen and which did just that. One evening, a well-known and highly respected media figure rang (or rather *tried* to ring) BBC Television News to warn of a possible misinterpretation of two opinion polls. We shall refer to the caller only by the initials BW.

BW's nightmare began after asking the BBC switchboard operator to put him through to the Television News Editor. Whereupon he was asked: "Who's calling?"

This information was provided, followed by a moment's silence. The switchboard operator informed BW that there was no answer, that News was far too busy preparing the News: "It is news time," he was told in no uncertain terms. BW was aware of that. It was the content of the bulletin that he wanted to talk to them about. "They haven't got time to talk," he was then informed. His request to be put through to the newsdesk was followed by another pregnant pause. Then: "This is the Duty Office, may I help you?"

BW told the Duty Office that he was trying to get through to the newsroom. "Who are you?" he was asked flatly. He obliged, giving his name and that of the equally well-known organisation he represented. "Are you giving news?" he was asked. "Can I help you?" BW responded in the negative on both counts, adding only that it was about an erroneous interpretation of a particular news item that he didn't want to see included in the later bulletin. But to no avail. News was busy and could not be disturbed. "No wonder people think the BBC is arrogant!" BW responded angrily. At which point he was asked not to shout and the line went dead. After having to call back he was greeted this time by a woman he described as 'unidentified.' She asked who was calling and could she help. BW told her that she was the third person to ask him that but even so he again gave his name and that of his organisation. "You can't speak to news now," he was told, "they are busy."

By now really angry, BW took the Lord's name in vain and begged the woman to put him through to the newsdesk. There was a pause, then came a familiar voice informing him (patronisingly): "This is the Duty Officer. May I help you? I understand you have been rude to our operator." BW then asked gently for the man's name, upon which he was told triumphantly: "We do not give our names." At which point BW gave up.

Seething and contemplating letters to the DG and the Chairman, or both, BW suddenly remembered that the editor of *The Listener* had asked him to do the Langham Diary next week. And who could resist such a story? Certainly not BW. Nor did he for it appeared in all its glory much as above. Maybe it was six of one and half a dozen of the other. But no matter, the reputation of the BBC lost out. Badly. Even so, in those days you really had to push the bad behaviour boat out in order to reap any form of meaningful punishment. But our friend managed to go the distance.

One evening, a few months after his altercation with BW, the same Duty Office Assistant was deep into a particularly pugnacious clash; this time with the Deputy Editor of a very popular daily tabloid, and one particularly ill-disposed towards the BBC. Undaunted by the potential consequences to himself and his employer, our man was unable, unwilling even, to give any ground or to concede the error of his ways. He preferred instead to battle on to score what he considered to be points. Suddenly the room became peaceful. He sat there quietly looking at one of the TV monitors with a sickly grin plastered across his face, blissfully unaware of the calls stacking up and waiting to be answered.

Minutes later came the dramatic entrance into the room of the Presentation Editor. This was the most senior person on duty after business hours. In those days it fell to him or her to pick up on any calls of complaint about Duty Office staff. Shaking with rage, the 'Pres. Ed' took one look at the obvious culprit and asked if he had taken a call from the Deputy Editor of a certain popular newspaper. The Assistant looked blank and muttered something inaudible. Exasperated, the Presentation Editor explained that the caller had rung off after gaining the distinct impression that the telephone had been placed in either a waste bin or a desk drawer. The Assistant offered a little chuckle, muttered something about insanity and shrugged. No sooner had Presentation Editor withdrawn than was the handset from the Assistant's desk drawer. The last confirmed sighting of this chap was on a miserable afternoon when he cheerily reported for duty, even though he had been told days earlier that his services were no longer required.

THE HOTLINE OF SHAME

One Sunday tabloid newspaper once informed its readers that it was 'possibly guilt' that made the BBC and other broadcasters keep records of telephone calls. The BBC, it claimed, maintained 'a pair of employees, trained to unnatural patience, like lunatic asylum attendants' to record in the 'duty officer's log-book' the views of those 'with sufficient energy or ire to ring up'. This 'log book' was then dutifully circulated 'to producers and similar functionaries who would rather not be troubled.'

All calls were (and indeed are) 'logged' and circulated for the edification of the wider BBC. The daily (or duty) Logs as they are known, are as much useful daily barometers of reaction as they are dubious platforms for eccentric opinion. Their usefulness depends solely on how they are viewed by those who read them and those who contribute to them. In this, science and cynicism go hand in hand. As a completely random, non-scientific daily round-up of the views, opinions and thoughts of a couple of hundred out of a total of 50-odd million viewers and listeners, it is a meaningless exercise.

A straw poll taken on a rainy winter's night in a phone box on the Isle of Muck would enjoy more resonance at a national level. Yet, 'The Log' in all its incarnations and infinite varieties has played a substantial part in helping make the BBC what it is.

At Broadcasting House the Daily Log was always regarded as a more serious document. Radio people tended to treat its contents with more respect, whereas the Television Log was considered more a bit of fun; a passing amusement at the start of the day. Or as a treasure trove of material for public access programmes such as *Points of View*. The Television Log might be filled with hundreds of calls about, say, political bias on the News or suchlike, but *Points of View* would invariably go for the likes of the man who objected to 'a nude bloke' he'd seen in a programme who was 'hung like a donkey' and would doubtless 'give a complex to other men!" Or the correction logged for the *Nine O'Clock News* pointing out that the Japanese city of Kobe is pronounced Ko-Bay, not Ko-Bee as 'Ko-bee is Japanese colloquial for having sex.'

Before the advent of new technology the salient points of calls (no matter how protracted) were furiously scrawled by hand across a pad of A4. As soon as a mini-novella had been compiled, the process of 'logging in' would begin. This entailed each Assistant in turn giving way to the task hour by hour across an 18-hour day to create the day's Log. Along one wall of the

Television Duty Office lurked a long table upon which lived two manual typewriters. Into each one at the start of the day was placed a virgin template for BBC 1 in one and for BBC-2 in the other. Ideally, all comments for the same programme were to be placed together under the one heading. Nowadays we take for granted the ability to cut and paste or input into a shared document. Prior to the advent of the personal computer, however, there were only two basic elements available in the creation of the Daily Log: communication and Sno-pake.

Imagine then, a team of two or three each with a batch of complaints about the length of *Blue Peter* presenter Sarah Green's skirt. As soon as one member of the team had entered their calls, the cry would go out: "Any more for Sarah's skirt?" An affirmative would require the leaving of an amount of space for others to add their stockpile. Eventually, before moving on to log comments for subsequent programmes, a final cry would go out: "any more for Blue Peter?" If there were none then it was deemed safe to proceed onto the next programme. Inevitably, Sod's law would dictate that there would always be someone, somewhere out there, who would ring in hours later to complain about Sarah's skirt. If the judicious use of Sno-pake failed to squeak another 'disgusted from Dewhurst', then *Blue Peter* would reappear later in the Log as '*Blue Peter (Continued)*' on the wrong side of the *Nine O'Clock News* and quite possibly again as *Blue Peter* (Further to) after *The Late Show*.

In time the two typewriters gave way to what was lavishly described as a word processor. By today's standards it was little more than a toy, but at the time it represented a real leap forward in the high technology stakes. Whereas the restraints of a single machine created new problems, at least late entries could be inserted as and when, with no more use for Sno-pake (except, of course, for the Assistant who was once found painting it onto the screen).

Kit resembling personal computers didn't arrive until the early 90s. Sadly the first system was a second hand pile of pants. Barely a single document could be processed without the most excruciating trials and tribulations. The system crashing at Broadcasting House over a weekend meant finding a security officer to open up the BBC's offices at 4 Cavendish Square. Here lived something called 'The Server'. Onto this mysterious object was pasted instructions on how to 're-boot the system'. Many a member of staff was mentally damaged as a direct result of this first encounter with new technology. As was many a server when the directive to 're-boot' was taken literally.

Heads of departments and other senior managers jealously guarded the contents of the Logs. Programme makers (the very people who should have) rarely, if ever, got to see the reaction generated by their programmes. That said, those that did manage to get hold of copies of the Log often made the case for keeping them strictly confidential. Like the presenter of a particularly mischievous BBC-2 satirical programme in a revealing rant published in the London evening *Standard* headlined **Bad-mouthing the barking viewers**. The constant stream of complaints about his show regularly appearing on the Daily Log, he opined, made the programme 'one of the most vilified around.' Whereas, he argued, the average 40 calls of complaint logged each week represented 'less than 2/1,000ths of a per cent' of the programme's measured audience.

Because of what he described as the 'ludicrous' nature of these calls', a number of the presenter's friends had all telephoned him to ask if in fact he had made the calls himself. This was a natural enough assumption as he once unleashed such a convincing tirade against his own Radio 1 show that he complained himself off the air. Further, he maintained, complaints to the BBC were 'quite rightly' ignored as 'they are all so palpably absurd'. Flicking through the Logs for any programme will reveal the same 'insane allegations and barkingly excessive language.' In the case of his own show, it had been variously described as "revolting", "absolutely disgusting" and "repulsive".

Should anyone be in any doubt as to the true meaning of these words, then they were treated to a highly graphic explanation. Readers were asked to imagine themselves on a crowded tube train when someone sneezes into your mouth, then to 'remember how it felt'. Now, that's revolting, disgusting and repulsive. People that complain, the presenter banged on, represent no one but themselves. Often what they say can reveal far more about themselves that the programmes they lambaste. Bothering to complain at all, in fact, betrayed a deeply suspect need for complainers to 'define their relationship with their television or radio'. Hmmm.

It was then revealed that complaining to the BBC was a 'fix'. This could be reported with some authority as the presenter had interviewed people who had complained. Not only had he 'found their brainpans full of cack', but far worse. Controllers, Heads of Department and others who daily read the Log cared little if anything about what viewers and listeners had to say. Senior BBC managers only reacted to complaints from above or from opinion formers. The only chance of the public's view attaching any credibility would be when it coincided with a decision already made. That said, contacting the BBC was not always an altogether wholly negative exercise - provided what was said was by way of appreciation. Then producers would fight tooth and nail for a share of any praise recorded.

In conclusion, the sole purpose of recording complaints was therefore quite obvious; to stop programme-makers thinking up 'real programmes' as opposed to Public Access offerings such as radio's *Feedback* and television's *Points of View*. These, according to the Oracle, served no purpose other than to fill holes in the schedule and to give employment to 'a smug git to pretend to take them seriously.' The presenter's venom spent, 'we are broadcasters', he declared, '0.0016 per cent of our audience is mad, and we don't give a Tonbridge toss.'

*

The vast majority of other presenters, producers and programme makers never got to see what the punters had to say about them and their products. Those that did were served via an illegal Log sub-distribution network, or leaks to the papers. Headlined **'Barking in Bordon'**, extracts from the Television Log once found their way into the Diary of a national broadsheet. Revealed was a 'surreal list' of comments from 'Mr Crazy and Mrs Angry' such as why there were so many Irish presenters on TV and why weather presenters waffle when all we want is the forecast?' The Diary reported this as typical of the sort of business conducted 'by the long-suffering staff of the BBC duty office.' One call was from a chap in Bordon, Hampshire. The programme *Rough Justice* had made reference to this town as being 'drab'. According to the caller, this passing remark had managed to lower house prices in Bordon by 10 per cent. Such is the power of television. All in all, the BBC's 'Duty Log' was found to be 'infinitely more entertaining than the average BBC sitcom.'

On more than one occasion journalists have used highly partial samplings drawn from leaked copies of the Log to tell their readers what to think about the BBC and its programmes. One tabloid in particular emphasized the confidential nature of the Log and how 'strongly held points of view had always remained a closely guarded secret.' But now, for the first time, readers could find out first hand what viewers really thought. If a copy of the Log littered with examples of anti-government bias laced with low moral content was sought, then that which fell into the hands of the *Daily Mail* could not have been bettered.

Headlined **The Hotline Of Shame**, readers were informed that of a total 237 calls logged, 'a staggering 83 callers rang to complain and only 54 rang with praise'. A ratio of complaints to appreciations of less than two to one is no mean achievement, but why spoil a good story? The focus of attention was on those licence payers who had 'hit out' specifically at 'anti-establishment bias' or were 'angered by scenes of sex and violence' particularly at unsuitable times. The trawl netted examples of 'Marxist propaganda', 'Left-Wing rubbish' and other 'disgusting and sadistic filth' spewed out by the BBC. Six callers objected to the presence of recently disgraced Conservative MP Cecil Parkinson on the panel of *Question Time*. His 'low moral standards' were considered not representative of Tory values.

It was a mere five years ago that the BBC was blessed with email. Until then, the distribution of the Log was an object lesson in sheer tedium. At the end of a 12 hour shift, each of the 20 plus pages were photocopied as many as eighty times (photocopier and God willing). Then each copy was stapled together and stuffed into individual envelopes for overnight distribution. This process was known as 'stapling and stuffing'.

I was stuffing at the end of what I thought was to be my last shift in the Duty Office. I did indeed escape, for a while, but as a wise man once said: 'as one door closes another slams in your face'.

SORTING IT

In January 1988 I was part of a small team whose job it was to stick microphones under the noses of the famous and the fatuous. We were known as Radio Trails. This was a somewhat quirky adjunct to Television Trails, except that we produced much the same product but in sound in order to promote television programmes on the radio. A good idea, I guess. Unless you happened to be a local radio station already struggling for an audience and forced to promote a TV alternative.

At this time, there wafted into Auntie's lounge a new breed of powercrat, quite untypical of regular BBC types. Deeply shrewd and scalpel-sharp, hugely entertaining yet daunting in their determination, enter the purely political wing of the BBC. Amongst other diversions, they were about radical changes to the coalface of accountability itself. The first casualty was the Television Duty Office Manager. The arrangement was amicable enough but it did leave the problem of who would fill his shoes. Then one fine day I was 'asked' to attend an informal interview.

41

This I didn't need. For on the day in question my mind was reeling with the prospect of interviewing Alan Whicker. After all, what questions do you ask a man who has asked them all? I performed inadequately at the informal interview before making a mad dash to Broadcasting House where I sat in Reception nursing a pair of profusely sweating palms. It came as something of relief when the Receptionist called over to inform me that Mr Whicker was unable to make it. The relief however was short-lived. I was told that he wanted to do the interview in his suite at the Dorchester Hotel. A cab was on its way to take me there.

How I wished I'd made more of an effort with my wardrobe that day. We journeyed to Mr Whicker's suite in a lift you could comfortably inhabit. Soon, my porcelain white knuckles were nervously rapping against a matching door. Seconds later the Grand Inquisitor himself beamed a genuine smile and ushered me in. That deliciously awful moment of no return. *I* was about to interview *him; He* that had only the Second Coming to include on his dance card. Was I nervous? Were my bowels telling me something? In a word: no. It was like some say: try to imagine the focus of your fear either naked or on the toilet. Suffice to say, my imagination needed little such stimulus. For the great man sat directly opposite me clad in nothing more than a very revealing towelling bathrobe.

Nevertheless, he ate me alive. As a conversation piece it wasn't bad. As a two-minute Radio trail it was a nightmare. For neatly inserted into every second word was a promotional reference to his latest book. Later, back in the studio I was deep into the process of filleting out these references when I was visited by one of that morning's interview panel. He offered his commiserations, to which I replied genuinely that it was OK. I didn't want the job anyway. That much was evident I was told; hence the commiserations. Despite my best efforts, I had been selected for the job of Television Duty Office Manager with immediate effect and until such time as it was decided to merge the job with that of the Duty Officer at Broadcasting House.

Now this idea made a certain amount of sense. Except that at that moment in BBC history, it was akin to combining the job of the *Tatler* Letters Editor with that of the *Sunday Sport*. Interviews for the new job of Information Officer were held some months later in 'The Panelled Room' at Number 4 Cavendish Square. This was the home of the BBC's Information Division and it was here, according to legend, that Lady Hamilton entertained Lord Nelson. The Panelled Room was indeed (once) a fabulous room, except for the MFI sink unit, the exterior wiring and plumbing and the tasteless furnishings accrued over decades of BBC tenancy.

Sunk into the listed 18th century panelling was screwed and nailed a chaotic assembly of bookshelves. The building's only untouched period feature was the impressive Grindling Gibbons staircase. Mercifully this had been spared the requisite layers of thick off-white gloss paint that had been liberally plastered elsewhere. This much I remember. Recollections of the interview are best forgotten. Suffice to say I was selected as Information Officer. These being the days before the luxury of an induction process, my introduction to this new world consisted of two minutes with the Head of Corporate Affairs. He outlined what he wanted and then commanded me in no uncertain terms to: "Sort it!". Next I met his deputy who left me in no doubt about the terms and conditions: "You fuck up, you fuck off!"

The next six weeks involved a crash course in how to be a New BBC manager. With no off-the-shelf training packages and without the luxury of time, many hours were spent in one-to-one sessions with he that was known as 'The Hatchet Man'. For hours we would sit together in one of the attic rooms at 4 Cavendish Square watching John Cleese training videos, roll-play interviewing techniques, acting out disciplinary or counselling sessions and anything else to help me employ, deploy and dump. Then there were the visits around the new empire. I had only ever encountered The BBC Duty Officer on the telephone. I had yet to visit the actual lair.

THE BEST LITTLE CLUB IN TOWN

Once, the BBC Duty Office *was* Broadcasting House. The transition therefore into the Information Division was greeted with more than a drop of incredulity. Both disciplines embraced a mindset, a methodology and even a social accord quite outside each other's experience and understanding. A Friday evening might see The Duty Office filled with furs and dress suits as a particularly fashionable Duty Office set sipped gin and tonic from the hospitality cupboard before embarking on a weekend in 'Devonshire'. Despite the horror of it all expressed by the new overlords, it was both fascinating and delightful.

Here was the place that shielded the Director-General from the more difficult callers demanding to speak to him. All the while some very distinguished people might be sitting in the adjoining 'Drawing Room', such as an ex-prime minister, a member of the royal family, business tycoons or stars of stage and screen. One morning, while I was enjoying a café cognac with the Duty Officer there came a sound in the corridor like that of a loaded milk float on cobblestones. "Excellent timing!"

declared the Duty Officer as he sprang to his feet to open the door. Immediately the room was filled with the clatter of glass against metal as a huge cage was rolled in, stacked to the gunnels with the contents of a modest off-licence. This was the weekly hospitality shipment. It became clear how the Duty Office earned its reputation as 'The Best Little Club in Town'.

There were only two members of staff that actually held the rank of Duty Officer. They were on duty around the clock together with 'the gal' who worked regular office hours. Supplementing this meagre workforce was a pool of part-time ex-senior BBC staff who provided cover 'in times of need'. Within this colourful contingent ranked a former Head of Radio 2, an ex-Senior Engineer and an octogenarian who used to read *Listen With Mother*. Other 'Casual Reliefs' would pop in 'to do a couple of hours here and there' between *other* social or charitable engagements.

Irrespective of the antiquated nature of the operation, it was deemed desirable to maintain much of the tradition for two reasons. Firstly as a sop to BBC Radio who were still smarting from the takeover of the Duty Office by the Information Division. This long established inner sanctum was seen as much an operational requirement as part and parcel of the ambience of Broadcasting House itself. BBC Radio was reasonably happy, provided that The Duty Room continued to function much as had done before, and at the same time managed to take more 'nuisance' telephone calls (those from the public) away from production areas. Now this was fine if the place was to be properly resourced, which it most definitely was not.

There was just the one typewriter, which was primarily the domain of the junior assistant, or 'The Gal'. This left the Duty Officer to operate at a higher level, such as entertaining a guest in the Drawing Room. The daily Log was known as the 'Crits & Apps', which was shorthand for the Daily Record of Criticisms and Appreciations. It never endured the notoriety of its Television counterpart, nor enjoyed its brevity. Entries were fulsomely recorded for the delight and edification of both senior management and the Duty Officers themselves. Mostly, the Duty Officer would draft entries by hand into a ledger which was then handed to 'the gal' to be typed up. As well as a daily round up of 'Crits and Apps' there was also, for some obscure reason long lost to history, a Weekly edition. While production of the Television Duty Office Log could merit the term quaint, the complexities of the Radio Log beggared belief.

Legend has it that in the early days of the last war, Winston Churchill rang Broadcasting House to make an inquiry. After his call had been variously re-routed he made a 'kind request' for a better system. And it was this that resulted in the birth of the Duty Office. The Duty Officer was to stand-in for the Duty

Controller to provide an emergency channel of communication with government departments, especially out of hours. Documents affecting evacuation, gas procedures and the like were kept in the Duty Room, which acted as the emergency headquarters for 'Controllers at need'.

The last time the Duty Room was used as an emergency operations centre was the day that President Kennedy was assassinated. Lesser post war 'emergencies' included the time when a lost pair of the BBC chef's trousers turned up in a ladies' toilet. Or when the Duty Office was called upon to guard Ernest Marple's bicycle. It was feared that this preferred perambulation of the deeply unpopular 60s Transport Minister might be attacked by pin-sticking, valve-removing members of staff. At such times, the Duty Officer would keep the Director General and other senior BBC staff informed and ensure that 'suitable action' was taken at all times.

As the recognised point of reference for all telephone enquiries from the public on all BBC matters, a clerk was employed to handle calls during office hours. Until 10.30 pm the Duty Officer was assisted by a relief who helped in the handling of calls and correspondence, requests for programme information and 'emergency typing at need'. Apart from what was described as a 'bath gap' in the early morning, the Duty Room telephones were never left unmanned. Aside from its wartime responsibilities, not a lot had changed when I arrived for my first fact-finding mission in 1988.

Then there was the infamous Home Telephone Numbers List. This harped back to the halcyon days when Broadcasting House was seen as a great ocean liner and the Duty Officer very much the ship's Purser. Comprising an unwieldy collection of tattered loose-leaf files and dog-eared pocket notebooks, work had been going on for decades to sort this 'vital senior manager resource'. But the system was never considered too broke when it came to the question of finding some money to fix it. Of the wide variety of potentially lethal Duty Office situations, this onerous task was particularly tricky.

The rule was never, but never, issue a home telephone number without first checking the staff number of the enquirer (yes, even if it was DG) and then asking for their telephone number to call them back. This wasn't, as one enraged senior executive blustered, an irksome case of jobs-worth, but a necessary double check on the identity of the enquirer. As can be imagined, effectively refusing a direct instruction for a home number from an insistent and highly agitated BBC supremo took some nerve. But with the best will in the world, there could be no guarantee that it *was* a BBC boss doing the demanding. Besides, the alternative didn't bear thinking about. The handing over of DG's number to a tabloid reporter, for example. One big-wig in particular was very nearly given a Filo-Fax one Christmas, fully loaded with all the names and numbers he requested with annoying regularity.

Apart from appeasing Radio management, much of the Duty Office tradition was retained as a public relations exercise. There were those opinion formers to consider who appeared regularly on influential radio programmes or as guests of the BBC. The main focus of attention was on the politicians who were able to see for themselves the BBC's coalface of accountability in action. They would either sit in the Drawing Room sipping a cup of tea or downing a gin and tonic, or whatever else took their fancy, or hover in the Duty Room listening in on the weird and wonderful business of the day. Nothing wrong in that you might think, except for the inherent difficulties in trying to appease Peter at the expense of Paul.

Before the takeover by Information Division far fewer calls were passed through the Radio Duty Office and so the business of 'receiving guests' was a generally more realistic affair. Consider then a lone member of staff attempting to placate double the number of difficult callers while at the same time politely gesticulating to a government minister, a business tycoon or a film star to go and make themselves comfortable in the Drawing Room.

On one occasion the singer Barry Manilow arrived unannounced. He was greeted by an astonished Assistant who was at the time dealing with a lengthy call. All she could think of doing was to place her hand over the mouthpiece and whisper to one of the biggest singing stars at the time, "do you want to go to the toilet?" Possibly he could see she was busy. Or maybe he is just that kind of guy. But he just smiled and went out again to find the nearest loo. A small search party found him later, lost somewhere deep within the bowels of Broadcasting House.

The Duty Office was in fact a suite of three rooms located on the east side of Broadcasting House along what is now the entrance to the Heritage Corridor. Dripping in shabby elegance, the 'Duty Room' itself was for most part bedecked by 1960s illuminated translucent pains of white plastic panels set into beams of rich, well-oiled wood. The office furniture was large and impressive. None more so than the Duty Officer's desk which occupied much of the space. Set behind the desk was a cavernous chair of equal proportions, flanked by an elegant standard lamp and a large electric fire complete with flickering imitation logs. Opposite was a smaller desk where sat the Assistant. Between them both was a mobile drinks cabinet that opened up like a tulip to reveal sufficient stock to satisfy even the most discerning tippler.

The hospitality cupboard itself was set into the far wall. Apart from all the drink, it also housed the BBC monogrammed silver plate, the bone china, crystal and other artifacts. Piled high in the same cupboard was a decent collection of beautifully cast, heavy glass ashtrays; indeed they were well used for this purpose and always appreciated. It was only some years later that it was discovered they were actually surplus to requirements pavement insets that used to run along Langham Street, which had once given light to the rather grim toilets below.

The Drawing Room was divided from the Duty Room by a wall of wood and glass. Near camouflaged into this minor work of art was a pair of matching doors. The Drawing Room was where the great and the good enjoyed the renowned hospitality of the Best Little Club in Town. Flanked on three sides by comfortable seats that matched the plush royal blue carpet, an army of polished brass table and standard lamps were dotted around the room, supplemented by banks of discreet inlaid lighting. A small door then led into a tiny corridor off of which lay The Bedroom. Here, after the last guest had staggered off home, the Duty Officer would retire for the night. Bedroom is perhaps too extravagant a word to describe a six by ten square feet of space. Neatly equipped with a bunk, a slim wardrobe, a sink and, of course, a telephone, it was effectively a cabin. The Purser's cabin.

*

My next port of call was the Programme Correspondence Section (PCS). This had also been taken over by the Information Division. To spend a day here, someone once wrote, 'is to spend a day in a world where the meaning of the expression *Auntie BBC* becomes immediately obvious, and where the people who write seem to address a relative, just like a faintly distant, somewhat elderly, maiden aunt.'

For nigh on 65 years the BBC's Programme Correspondence Department remained preserved in aspic, its traditions and values passed down from one head of department to another. Before the takeover, PCS nestled comfortably within the folds of that mysterious zone known as 'Registry'. This was a rambling department that acted as the buffer zone between the BBC and its direct dealings with the public. Throughout its entire existence, PCS maintained a somewhat dignified distance from the rest of the BBC.

Another observer once described the staff as an 'unusually dedicated; curiously isolated group, well away from programme-making yet in the front-line of its defence'. The BBC Handbook for 1928 observed: 'some misguided person once originated a rumour that the Programme Correspondence Section of the BBC is a home of lost illusions, inhabited by dreary people of suicidal tendencies, professing a peculiar cult of Pure Pessimism.'

So it was in this context, that I set out to meet the new relatives.

THE HOME OF LOST ILLUSIONS

Isolated it was. PCS occupied what was effectively a large upstairs flat in a characterful old building suitably situated in the centre of the village atmosphere of Marylebone High Street. The precarious journey to the top floor was by means of an ancient motorized metal cage. Waiting for me at journey's end was a nervous young woman who had been dispatched to ensure that I made it safety from the cage to a bolted and barred door opposite. The slight curtsey and lowered eyes of my greeter was at the same time as flattering as it was disconcerting.

What awaited me on entry was the complete corollary of the Duty Offices. The continual din of the telephones, televisions, breaking stories from the newsroom or wind from the Drawing Room was replaced by an atmosphere of ordered silence. Only the subdued clatter of manual typewriters, the rustle of paper and feint whisperings within a series of screened-off stable-like enclaves disturbed the tranquility of the place. I was neatly parked by a large central desk, which was strategically placed to survey the entire floor space. Here I was introduced to the three key players. Reminiscent of that scene from Macbeth, each of the three women were addressed as 'Miss' by members of staff sporadically appearing from their writing bins to submit pieces of work for approval, or not. But this was as nothing.

After a brief tour, I was taken to a separate, inner sanctum where lived the Secretary to the Head of the department. She in turn gently rapped on her boss's door before gingerly opening it. "Ye-ays?" came a clipped retort, highly reminiscent of Joyce

Grenvile, from within. On the command of "Eynt-orrr", I obediently made my way into a spotlessly clean and numbingly tidy half acre. It was also stiflingly hot. This wasn't surprising as all the windows were sealed with tape. "So v'ey nayce to meet you, Ayed," beamed the Head of PCS genuinely, leaning across for the merest touch of my fingers with her gloved hand. I felt unclean and unworthy, but I needn't have worried unduly. For as we sat sipping tea from cups so delicate that they bulged from the weight of their contents, I was treated to a rogue's catalogue of those not very nice 'Information people' that had suddenly appeared on the scene, upon whom was poured the full weight of her not inconsiderable scorn and loathing.

The 'role' of Head of Programme Correspondence, I learned, was a mantle that carried a heavy commitment. It could and did so easily 'ruin one's listening and viewing enjoyment', for 'one was always on the look-out for anything which might bring in further caseloads'. Letters requiring 'special attention', perhaps policy-based, simply *had* to be dealt with at this senior level. Appropriate advice was taken *only* from Broadcasting House. There had been the MI5 vetting scandal. This involved the sinister occupant of a mystery office at Broadcasting house, placed, allegedly, to ensure only 'the right sort' ran the BBC.

Then there had been the *Real Lives* programme *At the Edge of the Union*, which dealt with the extremes across the political divide in Northern Ireland. This was the programme that provoked Prime Minister Thatcher to famously demand that terrorists should be "denied the oxygen of publicity". It also led to a 24-hour strike by BBC and ITN journalists following the BBC Board of Governors' decision to pull the programme. After much unwelcome public wrangling it was eventually broadcast, leaving viewers to wonder what the fuss was all about in the first place.

Otherwise, the rest of the 10,000 letters each week were allocated to six Assistant Letter-Writers. Each of these Assistants had to have a detailed knowledge of the BBC and its output. With the help of their own clerical support teams, they were able to answer most letters either from personal knowledge, or through close liaison with producers. Sometimes the mail sack would contain weird and wonderful things, such as throat pastilles for the announcers, or live insects in matchboxes for identification by the BBC's Natural History Unit in Bristol.

Even the variety of stationery used was bizarre. As yet there had been nothing written on toilet paper, but letters could arrive on anything from good quality parchment to ceiling-lining paper; from the backs of envelopes to pages torn from school exercise books. Once an entire letter was contained on the back of a tape measure that had to be opened out to read it. Badly addressed mail to the BBC was no problem for PCS. Letters addressed to 'Mr Jones, BBC, London', or 'Olly Onion, c/o The Basket, Munch Bunch Village, TV Land' would be found the right home. Likewise at Christmas with hundreds of letters addressed to Santa. Here replies were sent out with an assurance that 'Santa Claus is very busy just now so he has asked me to reply on his behalf....'

A Programme Enquiry Unit answered some 300 letters a day about past and present BBC programmes. Quite often anything of quality broadcast was 'bound to be the BBC', which was a nice compliment, but a real bind when attempting to disentangle the actual source. Sometimes expectations ran to the extreme with one flabbergasted ITV enquirer declaring 'well, it all comes out of the same box, doesn't it?' Of the more unusual requests there was the security firm who wanted the name and address of a good burglar to help test their systems. But the strangest request of all time came from the man who collected toe-nail clippings of famous personalities. In pursuit of this unsavoury hobby he included with his letter a bunch of little plastic bags. Quite how extensive that particular collection was (or is) is not known, nor how many personalities actually contributed to it.

Most enquiries were dealt with by means of a vast card index system numbering over half a million cards. These were once the sole domain of the wonderfully titled 'Card Ladies'. Because they were unable to type, their decision-making abilities were highly suspect. Letters requiring only an acknowledgement or a simple reply were duly marked up and dispatched to the three Card Ladies who would then match the code to one of an assortment of some 30 different postcard responses.

A straightforward acknowledgement stated plainly:
Thank you for your recent letter, to which attention will be given.

Whereas a more considered reply simpered:

An appreciation is always welcomed but this is to tell you, albeit in printed form, how happy those concerned were to receive your kind comments, and in the hope that you will continue to enjoy many more years of happy broadcasting.

The Christmas of 1989 saw out the last ever Programme Correspondence Festive Mince Pie Party. Despite the department's splendid isolation, this annual event had for decades attracted the very highest profile guests, including the Chairman and the Director-General. Stars and celebrities of the day all made the annual pilgrimage in order to give thanks. The 'gels' were required to be on their feet at all times; attentive to guests and under strict orders not to slurp their coffee. They were not allowed drink, nor to drop a single crumb if they partook of a mince pie. Come the New Year, the last Head of PCS took her leave. The department was renamed Viewer & Listener Correspondence (VLC) in line with the new BBC ambitions.

THE UNSUNG HEROES OF BROADCASTING

Irrespective of all the changes being made to the coalface of accountability, public perceptions of the BBC remained the same. As far as the Licence Payer was concerned, there was the Duty Officer to call with a complaint or 'The BBC' to write to. As for the Press, opinion was divided. On the one hand, BBC current affairs programmes were always calling for more openness and more accountability in government, in the police, industry – everywhere in fact, except the BBC. The Duty Office was described as a facility 'so unhelpful it made directory enquiries sound like the Samaritans.' And reading the public's 'rubbish letters' was second only to 'the thrill' of writing a facetious reply'. On the other hand, telephoning the BBC to complain 'was for saddoes'.

Even so, one journalist found herself sufficiently irked to do so. After the 'duty officer' had logged her 'incensed ranting with a blank efficiency' she hung up. Purged of her rage, she was left with a feeling of guilt. She reflected on 'that poor woman, sitting solitary in a BBC cupboard, the blameless butt of every loony telly addict in the country'. And she thought that calling in was sad. So she came to see 'the cupboard' for herself and admitted to having got it all wrong. 'It's not all nutters and it's not all lonely women sitting in a cupboard with buns at the back of their heads, but a growth industry for young people doing a job that was so highly under-rated'. These were, in her opinion, 'the unsung heroes of broadcasting - next time, respect.' Somewhere between those widely differing perceptions lay the truth.

In its purest form, all that's required to answer telephone calls is a telephone and someone to pick it up each time it rings. If the telephone tends to ring a lot then more instruments are needed together with appropriate (and properly trained) numbers of staff to answer them. If the business is large and diverse, a switchboard or some form of switching system is installed to distribute calls to where they need to go. As the business grows so there must be an adequate spread of the right staff in the right places to deal the right calls at the right time. That is all there is to managing telephony.

Indeed that's exactly how it began for the BBC and how it failed to move on. By 1938 such was the demand for information by telephone that it gave rise to the Telephone Enquiry Bureau. This was the BBC's first official telephone service. At the end of a three-week intensive examination during which 23 'girls' were tested for general knowledge, tact and initiative, Rowena

Pratt and Gertrude Adcock were appointed. The number of calls varied from day to day, with no more than 15 an hour across a busy shift. The Telephone Enquiry Bureau was expected to be able to offer 'immediate answers' to all programme and BBC Service enquiries.

By 1940 the Duty Officer had become the point of reference for all unsolicited telephone calls from the public. That said, the switchboard continued to provide information or answers to basic programme questions. However, what was deemed to be the right levels of resourcing for the 1930s and 40s did not translate to life fifty years on. It might seem ludicrous in this day and age where new telephone lines can appear faster than a rash of calls following the cancellation of *Star Trek*, but in the BBC a decade ago it was a very big deal.

The integration of the Programme Correspondence Telephone Enquiry Clerk into the newly created Radio Information Office brought with it a very particular problem (sorry, challenge). There was no spare telephone line to answer the additional 100 calls per day. Within the spirit of the piece it was down to managers to find solutions and not present the BBC with problems. The Corporation had greater decisions to ponder than the provision of telephones. Whatever, another spare line had to be found before the dawn of the new Millennium. The solution began with a trip to John Lewis in Oxford Street.

After purchasing of the longest telephone extension cable available, this was then connected to the telephone socket in The Bedroom. It was then run under the door, through the Drawing Room out into the main office. Here it was re-connected to the former bedroom handset to become the new dedicated programme information line. The switchboard was specifically informed that this line would be active weekdays between nine and five for programme enquiries only. Of course, it rang incessantly at all hours with all sorts of calls. For within this emerging 'integrated and up-to-date package of customer services', the switchboard managers themselves were also required to improve their service. So, quite understandably, they seized upon any opportunity to place callers where and when they could.

It was long established custom & practice for switchboard staff to be armed with copies of *Radio Times* to provide basic programme information and transmission times. Also they were aware of repetitious pieces of information such as addresses given out after programmes. But this made little business sense and wouldn't even enter into a casual debate today. But ten years ago the BBC world was a very different place. Balancing 100,000 unsolicited calls a year across a mixture of compromise and local agreement was just common sense.

Unlike its Radio sibling, the Television Duty Office had always been more of an information factory so here there was less initial dramatic change. It worked to full capacity across an 18 hour day, seven days a week, 365 days a year. Calls were received via a small battery of post-Bakelite telephones at the disposal of an even smaller workforce. A single Assistant covered the *Breakfast Time* shift, which started at 5 am. This was reinforced by another shift at nine, with the team building up to a staggering four or five towards 4 pm. After 8pm there would be just two Assistants dealing mostly with comments and complaints until closedown. At weekends there were even less staff on duty.

Here, one casualty of the move into the Information Division was the loss of a beautifully bound collection of *Radio Times*. There was no question of replacing them when it was found that each volume cost something in the region of £250. Traditionally they were considered a vital resource, but in reality they satisfied little more than idle curiosity. *Radio Times* will always be very much the everyday workhorse at the coalface of accountability. No matter what processes and practices have come and gone over the past 70 years, one factor has remained constant throughout; as close to the hand as the telephone has to be a copy of 'the definitive programme guide'.

That said, once, what was actually printed in *Radio Times* often bore little resemblance to what actually appeared on the screen. Promotional trails for the magazine used to declare: 'If it's on – it's in'. Given the 'flexibility' of BBC scheduling however, cynics much preferred: 'If it's in – it's off'. And this where the duty office 'Master' came about. This was a single copy of the current edition of *Radio Times* into which would be written, stuck or pasted any change of programme or changes to the published transmission times. In effect it became the only truly definitive programme guide. So much so that it had other uses too.

The BBC once employed a team of retired ex-Scotland Yard CID officers as internal Investigators. It was their job to check out incidents of theft on BBC premises, as well as appearing as witnesses on behalf of the corporation in criminal trials. For example, where a suspected felon would cite what was on television as an alibi. This was considered a simple matter of checking out the appropriate back issue of *Radio Times* down at the local reference library.

To a magistrate it can sound pretty convincing to hear that on the night in question the accused was in fact watching a film on BBC-1 which clashed with a gardening programme on BBC 2, causing an almighty row between the accused and 'the wife' that went on for days (chuckles around the courtroom). And then to have produced in court a copy of *Radio Times* confirming absolutely his (or her) story. Now, the wiser lawyer would always double check with the broadcaster and here is where the Duty Office 'Master' would come into play.

The BBC Investigator had only to drop by the Information Office to check out the *Radio Times* Master for the day in question. Quite often there would be a variation – possibly, and not unusually - a sport overrun or a programme dropped for some reason. This information would then be double-checked with the Daily Transmission Log and before you could say 'it's a fair cop, guvnor,' chappie was duly banged to rights.

Although decimation of the published schedules happens less often these days, some things never change. During his recent trial, it transpired Lord Archer sent his secretary to check out *Radio Times* for what was on television the night of his alibi. But did she call the BBC to confirm that what was in was actually on?

By 1992, The Television Information Office had acquired space on a vital piece of customer care kit known as a Call Sequencer. Said item had been installed in Transport, the department responsible for providing cabs, bikes and so forth. It just so happened that sufficient spare capacity was available on the system to allow for another user. This meant that the system's not inconsiderable installation costs could be fully justified overnight and its annual maintenance charges halved. The Transport manager, who knew the value of a penny, was delighted, as indeed was the Information Division forever on the lookout for a good bargain.

With such a system it was found than even our profound lack of staff could be offset with customised greetings. Instead of inflicting callers with the dubious delights of mindless muzak, they were informed of alternative means of finding information or contacting the BBC. The beautifully modulated tones of a BBC continuity announcer added just that little bit of extra value for the price of a pint. For these were still the days when it was possible to do such things without having to draw up a Service Level Agreement or issue a charge code.

A batch of second hand telephone sets were acquired that seemed at the time the very essence of sophistication. As well as other tricks they allowed for the first time the operation to open up; increase or reduce the number of lines and to close down without having to rely on the switchboard to do it for us. This might not seem much, but even at its most basic level, anyone who has ever managed a telephone service will appreciate the ability to silence the shriek of an otherwise unoccupied instrument. But at the end of the day, it was all little short of a charade.

At the time of writing, the corporation is once again banging on about the concept of a 'One BBC'. This is something it does every decade or so, usually with the arrival of a new DG who must look around and wonder how and why it is all so unnecessarily complicated. Back in the 1990s for example, there was no such thing as The BBC Information Office. There was the Television Information Office at TV Centre and there was the Radio Information Office at Broadcasting House. These were two very different zoos representing and relating to two very different animals. The former Duty Offices could have shared much, but for over 30 years the thought never occurred. The notion of a 'BBC Information Office' was practically, logistically and geographically the product of pure stage management. This was fine, just as long as the punters never got to see backstage. Which, of course, as the BBC was becoming increasingly more accessible, they did.

To suggest that there was any love lost between *The Daily Mail* and the Corporation at this time would be something of a criminal understatement. So the idea of one of its columnist spending a day at the very coalface of accountability was greeted with a modicum of trepidation. 'You want to see it,' he reported, predictably less than impressed with the Television office. 'It has a few desks and six phones.' He was asked what he expected. 'Oh, something the size of an aircraft hangar with 200 people in shirt sleeves'. In fact there were just two people on duty – the regular quota after 8pm. 'Was this therefore the place of legend that daily received thousands of complaints?' The perplexed columnist was assured that this was indeed the place that received thousands of calls each week for information, or to make a comment. 'But these thousands of complaints you read about', he quizzed more in despair than disbelief. That old cliché about not believing everything you read in the 'papers, readily came to mind.

As it turned out, it wasn't a busy night and the level of staffing proved to be adequate. With such 'slack trade' in evidence, the columnist wondered why the BBC bothered to have a Duty

Office at all. And you could see his point. He had chosen a particularly quiet evening. In fact a very quiet evening. But then Ambulance crews and fire fighters get them too. It was rare but not necessarily extraordinary as the more fulsome Logs of less forgiving shifts bore testimony.

It was a very curious thing in that it was bound to be quiet if a journalist or a film crew was around to record the action; a bit like taking the car to the garage only for that funny noise to suddenly disappear. So much so, that consideration had been given to employing journalists on a rota basis. If the man from the *Mail* wanted to witness busy then he needed to be around when sport overran or *Neighbours* was dropped. Those were the times when we could have done with an aircraft hangar full of people.

*

By January 1993, the Programme Correspondence Section, now newly branded as Viewer & Listener Correspondence (VLC) had shifted from their comfy quarters at Marylebone High Street and into the new White City building. This ubiquitous grey metal lump was designed to be the BBC's new Corporate HQ, but it never quite captured the affection of the top brass. It can be experienced in all its dubious glory as you travel out of London along the Westway. The Information Offices then combined with VLC to form a new department known as Viewer & Listener Relations.

The Television Information Office moved again, this time to more permanent accommodation at TV Centre. The woodwork creaked in the heat, as did the staff when it was discovered the air conditioning ducts were not connected. But we had the window, which comprised one third of the goldfish bowl that passed for my office. If left wide open together with the main door, there was sufficient air. Just. Passers by stopped to gawp at our badge of office placed on the wall outside. "Information Office?" some would enquire. "Oh, you mean the Duty Office - the place where all the nutters ring in'.

The original plan to locate both Information offices on a single site was still on hold. The sensitivity of moving out of Broadcasting House was deemed well, too sensitive. An Overheads Review body had been set up to closely examine all the areas of the BBC not directly involved in making programmes. In this, the Information Office(s) and VLC then shifted sideways to form (yet another) new department called Viewer and Listener Information. Joining us in this new enterprise was the Engineering Information Department (EID), a surviving fragment of the old Engineering Directorate, once the most powerful in the BBC. That was until Japanese and other sophisticated technology became available 'off the shelf'. Increasingly there was considered to be less and less of a need for the BBC's backroom boffins to pioneer the very tools of broadcasting. Some of this expertise still exists, mainly in a large old country house in Surrey where white coats, clip boards and loud nylon shirts still perform the odd technical miracle.

Even by 1994, EID was a reasonably large outfit. Part of their work was to travel the length and breadth of the land in high-tech Range Rovers checking signals and curing reception faults. Much to their chagrin, the engineers were to join VLC in the White City building. Here they tested to the extreme the minimalism envisaged by the building's creators. It was not designed to suit the organised chaos of a BBC Engineer whose world demands clutter, equipment, wires, clutter, meters, measures, clutter, monitors, receivers, manuals and clutter.

The reason for this 'diplomatic amalgamation' was given as the 'common provision of information and a shared relationship with the Viewer and the Listener'. Even more tenuously it was claimed that the timing was 'magnificent', as the new department would now be much better able to address 'the particular difficulties presented by the Ball by Ball cricket commentary on Radio 4 (Long Wave).' In reality, Engineering Information had little in common with the work of the Information Offices and its new Correspondence colleagues, and vice versa.

EID's information provision tended to be less obscure. The technically challenged amongst us who have heard of such phenomena, might (and often do) cite cross-channel interference for affecting the quality of our TV picture. Crudely this is when the picture breaks up and blame is afforded a stray signal from another station. Whereas the real reason – especially during the late autumn months – can be due to 'a combination of growth in trees and their subsequent loss of leaves causing a stronger attenuation than previously'. And not a lot of people know that.

The Engineers were equally mystified about how their new pals managed to define some of their more outlandish requests. What, for example, could be done in the case of the *Newsnight* presenter 'constantly waving her pen around in the air like

Sooty's wand'? Or the lady from Devon who insisted that she much preferred the hard-hitting tele-interrogator Jeremy Paxman when he played the footman in *Upstairs Downstairs*. Or again the man who further complained that he would not have previously complained had friends and relatives explained to him sooner that *Knowing Me, Knowing you...with Alan Partridge* was a spoof and not a real chat show. But there was some common ground. Like those callers so stunned at the speed with which they received the answers to their questions that they would invariably disappear for ages while they went to find a pen and paper, or whatever it was they were reading which led to the call. Better still, like the man from Carlisle who, when asked for his name, replied: "Hold on – I'll just go and get it."

VLC staff had by now been without a manager for the first time in 70 years and the result was showing. The hundreds of letters arriving every day were carefully sorted and sifted. Then each carefully sorted and sifted batch was apportioned to one of seven strictly specialised units. Each of these units might clear perhaps a dozen carefully crafted pieces of correspondence each day. Whereas once a bulging In-Tray would have raised a plucked eyebrow, now creaking cupboards full of letters failed to attract even a sideways glance. Drastic action was called for in order to remedy what had become The Great Backlog of '94..

Action came in the form of a battalion of newly redundant ex-BBC folk, each supplied with a PC, a mountain of letters to rival Everest and an instruction to get it cleared. However, even those with many years public relations experience were shocked to discover that what might appease a government minister does not translate easily to Joe Public. Like the correspondent, deeply unimpressed with any of the current output on BBC Television, who wanted to know: 'Why don't you just go back to people shagging?' There was the man miffed to discover the reply to his original letter was printed on recycled paper. He wrote again to grumble about 'yet another BBC repeat'. And the woman who had been watching the feature film *Blind Date* and who wanted to know what had happened to Cilla Black. Or the particularly spooky serial abuser who added as a spine-chilling postscript to one of her multiple demands for celebrity photographs: '…Don't attach paperclips to the photo I want, which, I must receive, for eating purposes…'.

Then, in the middle of this came news of yet another 'diplomatic amalgamation'. Across the BBC whatever could be sold, hired or leased was disappearing faster than sporting contracts. A new buzzword had appeared in the BBC vocabulary: outsourcing. Nowhere was safe: from security to scenery; catering to cameramen; film crews to finance. Not even the BBC's complaints department. Libraries & Archives was another department that felt strongly that most of its functions were fundamental to programme making. However, unlike Viewer & Listener Information, a financial value could be placed on its activities. For example, a charge could be levied on the borrowing of a book or a CD.

The January (1995) edition of *Libraries & Archives News* was headlined: 'Welcome new colleagues!' The New Colleagues were us. 'Information supply is one of our core activities', explained the newly imported Libraries Czar. It made eminent sense therefore, to combine the activities of Libraries & Archives with Viewer & Listener Information. With immediate effect, all staff were instructed '**only**' ever to refer to the newly branded *Information* & Archives. Libraries staff reacted badly to this news. 'Somewhere', one wrote, 'there was a room full of "suits" sitting around all day with nothing to do but think up new titles for old jobs'. To this, folk at the coalface of accountability could seriously relate. As a footnote to the announcement, Correspondence staff and the Engineers were to be shipped five miles west to Ealing Broadway.

Villiers House is the highly visible monolith straddling Ealing Broadway station like a huge white upturned shoebox. Once the epitome of 1960s municipal, it had only recently been transformed into a moderately less offensive slab of contemporary architecture. It was destined to become the home of the BBC's financial services, but in the meantime offered shelter to a variety of itinerant departments such as Training, Recruitment, Programme Acquisition and now two thirds of Viewer & Listener Information.

A lot of effort had gone into exorcising the worst excesses of the building's era. It no longer had the feel of a tax office. It was bright, airy and packed with technological goodies such as lights that went off if you didn't move, and lifts that often did the same. It was convenient for the tube, subject to the foibles of signal failure at White City. It was conditioned to pump out cold air in the winter and to fail altogether during the few weeks of the year when the temperature soared into the 90s. And it boasted a canteen designed to baffle each and every concept of customer care. The modest BBC crest etched onto the glass entry doors was the only clue as to this being a 'BBC' building. It was an outpost; a B&B for homeless BBC folk; God's waiting room for the dispossessed. Or, dubbed in homage to the classic 60s horror film, *Village of the Damned*: 'Villiers of the Damned.' Personally, I didn't mind the place. But then I didn't have to work there. Or so I thought.

WHERE THE CUSTOMERS ALWAYS WRITE

It was coming up to March. When the days are short and the evenings long. Winter days and nights provide much greater scope for complaint that there is *"absolutely nothing* to watch", or for transmitters to buckle under the weight of bad weather thus guaranteeing nothing to watch at all. For a second time in as many years, Viewer & Listener Correspondence was having a tough time keeping its head above paper. The department had by now been without direct line management for going on three years, and the correspondence crew were set in their ways. It was too long a time to leave unattended such a dispirited and highly emotional group. Morale was zero. Motivation, understandably, was somewhere below that. It was against this backdrop that I was asked if I might like to go in and sort it.

Drastic action was required to get a handle on more missing mail than accredited the Great Train Robbery. The main problem was that for too long, too much time had been spent providing even the most questionable worldviews carefully considered responses. Every licence fee payer, irrespective of his or her views, has every right to expect a proper response from the BBC. But inordinate amounts of time were being spent on matters that had little or nothing to do with the BBC. Like the man who was wanted to know: 'If Odette was so badly tortured by Nazis – how come she has only just died at 82?' To this dubious conundrum was added, 'The BBC is affected by a terrible disease – a Jewish disease, most apt.'

Was this a rhetorical question or an observation? Actually determining what is and what is not the business of the BBC can be difficult where the cryptic meets brevity. One letter simply contained: 'I am confident I will experience no delay in receiving a reply from the adequately funded and staffed Viewer and Listener Correspondence Department, and I am sure all your posts are safe enough under this government.' Another stated: 'It's not a reply from you I want, but action from those responsible to pull up these standards which have sunk so low.' It was a fear of subsequent complaint that had left the correspondence staff feeling duty bound to cater for the needs of all, irrespective of their grip on reality.

What also created these backlogs was an inability to distinguish between answering a letter and entering into correspondence. The BBC is unable to express an opinion on matters other than broadcasting. It can help where it can or advise where help might be obtained from elsewhere (perhaps where that help is long overdue). Even Lord Reith understood that there would always be those determined never to be satisfied.

Particularly those who expect to deal directly and only with 'the top man' and not have their correspondence passed to one of his 'wretched little protectors'.

Inevitably disappointed on receiving replies from such a quarter, they demand explanations from the Chairman as to why 'an obsequious little person' had afforded them an answer. One such correspondent claimed to have written to the Pope and to have received a personal reply; 'why then could not the Director-General of the BBC proffer the same privilege?' Some might argue that he had a point. Others understand the limitations of time on top executives of any large organization (the Vatican excluded).

'One who will say or might be thinking something so ineffably arch', wrote one correspondent of a TV personality, 'that the rest of us in our swinish cloddery might not completely savour its Wildean drollness without a clue, so successfully has this coxcomb sucked his teeth in the public's face, so to speak'. This was typical of hundreds of unresolved files found languishing in cupboards and boxes throughout the fourth floor of Villiers House. Originally this correspondent was merely forwarding his view. He was making a comment not a complaint; a simple acknowledgement would have done. However, it was the 'Messianic missive received' that caused him to complain and in turn create a protracted bout of correspondence

A letter can contain criticism, but not necessarily complaint. Criticism can be couched in positive and constructive language. Complaints usually contain stronger, more negative language. Letters can also be argumentative without being complaints because complaints are more than just disagreements. They are objections to something broadcast and these are the ones requiring a highly specific response. But even then, there is no guarantee of success. To ensure that unrealistic expectations do not mushroom out of all proportion someone has to call a halt. One example had lasted half a year.

It began with a light-hearted quip from one of the nation's best-loved radio personalities about the most unlikely of garden objects. A letter of protest followed which was answered by VLC. Dissatisfied with the response, the complainant wrote to the Director General. Unhappy with that he then wrote to the Chairman. Continued attempts to satisfy eventually saw a now weighty case file on the desk of the channel Controller. Familiar with its contents, he then passed it onto the senior producer of the programme in question. 'I am amazed', he noted, 'that such an obviously reasonably intelligent person can have so seriously missed the point. Just our luck to have probably the only "serious student of wheelbarrows as a listener.' Had the initial and subsequent replies been as straightforward, then much time, energy and money would have been saved.

'VIP' correspondents mostly require exactly the same information as do lesser mortals. In fact, delays in replying to these letters can be exacerbated purely and simply by a House of Commons letterhead. Some people use their MP when writing to the BBC for the added gravitas. The BBC has always been a bit twitchy about dealings with MPs and the like, and so a highly convoluted process had evolved when it came to dealing with their letters. As a result, instead of aggrieved constituents jumping on the fast track, they often languished longer on the milk train through a mixture of nervousness, confusion and lack of clear ownership.

During one morning surgery, I came across the same correspondent's name attaching a whole series of mini-novellas. Each was stamped as having come from a range of senior BBC managers, Members of Parliament, the Secretary of State for the (then) Department of National Heritage and even the Prime Minister's office. This dossier, for that is what it had become, comprised a full nine months of time, effort, licence fee as well as taxpayers' money across the entire spectrum of public accountability.

Given a veritable Who's Who of the great and the good accumulated thus far, it was no wonder that this particular hot potato continued to be passed from pillar to post. And even less of a surprise that it should have been condemned to a VLC cupboard in the vein hope that it might go away. But what was surprising was that the core complaint had nothing to do with the BBC, nor any issue of public concern. Rather it was an object lesson in the power of an individual's determination not to be deterred by what they perceived as bureaucracy. But any sympathy, or indeed respect for such an indomitable spirit, was rapidly replaced with disbelief.

The theme throughout this saga was that the BBC 'from top to bottom was unwilling to help'. So too were the various elected officers of State, including the Heritage Secretary (described as 'obstructive' and 'unhelpful') and the Prime Minister's Office ('deeply disappointing'). So it was that the matter came back time and again to the BBC. For it was the BBC that had started this prolonged and extensive campaign. A lack of sympathy about having to pay the licence fee, or a failure to accept a serious lapse in standards would have been understandable. Indifference with regard to an incidence of gratuitous violence might have justified this level of discontent. But to complain that the BBC was not prepared to help find a particular knitting pattern manufacturer was something else.

This was an extraordinary example, but by no means unique. There are people who look upon the BBC as a personal resource. A combination of sheer bluster; threat and skilful articulation often creates more problems than can be solved. After all, it only takes one accident on an otherwise smooth flowing motorway to quickly create a gridlock. As far as VLC was concerned, the sooner the hard shoulder mentality was coned off the better. Learning when and how to say that hardest word in the English language ('No') soon saw an end to backlogs.

'I am not one for complaining', began another curious diatribe from Surrey, 'but I just could not tell you how upset I was after buying a packet of mini quiche from Waitrose'. It's not unusual for letters to the BBC to begin in this way; that is, on the surface to have little or nothing to do with the organisation. 'I have been in the catering business for over 50 years', the story unfolded, 'but I have never complained about anything. The mini quiches had no taste and after my friends tried one, they tried no more. It was money just thrown away, and for nearly £3 a packet. I don't think you will have customers coming back for more'.

It was assumed that the information provided was intended for *Watchdog* or some other consumer programme, to which copies were duly forwarded. This action was included in the subsequent reply together with the suggestion that Waitrose might themselves be keen to hear about the matter. A reasonable enough response by any standards, given the nature of the material. And indeed the correspondent wrote back to thank the BBC for such a 'fulsome response'. However, still concerned about the mini quiche issue, he added: 'I expect you are wondering why I wrote to you about this in the first place', which had indeed crossed the mind. 'Well', he explained, 'I was a window cleaner and in the catering trade. I carried on both for a time. For that reason I expect the BBC to take the necessary action'. Thus can be the difficulties in answering a letter and entering into correspondence.

FROM CRANKS TO CUSTOMERS

Ask anyone in the BBC world of today what is 'The Customer' and you might well be told that the BBC exists to serve him or her as the most important element of the business. Whether by telephone, letter, email or in person, customers no longer stifle the creative process, but are the purpose of it. There is no 'them and us' culture. The BBC is obliged by its reputation not only to meet, but to exceed its customers' high expectations. The organization is charged by its history, its traditions and its values to develop its people and practices in order to raise standards in an ongoing commitment to customer service excellence. To some this is still a very strange and suspicious form of language. To most but a few short years ago, it might as well have come from Mars.

The BBC as a whole has no huge problem buying-in to the customer service concept. It's when it comes down to that part of the organization that all too often gets lost in the politics - show business - that it becomes fuzzy. When putting on a show the audience is king. An audience comprises people who are watching or listening to something such as a play, a concert, a film or a television programme. The relationship is proactive, interactive and a little magical. It is difficult to perceive in the same way as that of service provider and customer. Continuity announcers address viewers or listeners when talking to the audience, not customers. Individual stars, disc jockeys, presenters, newsreaders and weather people have fans or admirers, not customers.

Along with all the other trappings of the nefarious nineties, the BBC needed to get fit in order to survive in the fast emerging dynamic world of digital. In this, viewers and listeners were to be known as customers. Mercifully, Birtspeak *Shareholders* and *Fundholders* never really took off, and references to 'those who *consume* BBC products', came and went with the blink of an eye. In fairness, while the terminology was a bit suspect the sentiment was sound. After all, even some senior BBC folk still regarded doing business with 'The Public' as a not altogether wholesome affair. On informing the Chairman who he was and what he did, the Head of the newly created Programme Complaints Unit was told, 'never mind, old chap, go and grab a large drink'

To a greater or lesser degree this attitude had always been rife throughout the Corporation. The BBC knew best and despised outsiders for criticising what it did and how it operated. Naturally this made its way to some of those representing the Corporation. Of the myriad initiatives rolled out and objectives to be met under the wing of Information & Archives, two in particular had a fundamental bearing on the brothers and sisters at the coalface of BBC accountability: '*The Benchmarking Exercise*' and '*Customer Focus.*' These initiatives were designed to establish if the department was delivering 'to customers value for money' and how it could 'identify customer opportunities for improving the services'.

The Benchmarking Exercise was straightforward enough. Numerous consultants were brought in to compare 'key target performance information' with other organizations. Except they never really found anything like a close match. A journalist once wrote that staff at the coalface 'could tell John Birt more about what his producers should be doing than the small army of management consultants he has employed at public expense'. For in order to focus on the customer, for example, required looking back in order to look forward. BBC History shows that in an organization where more wheels are reinvented than pound the motorways of Britain each year, particular elements remain constant. Not least the types of people that tend to call and write. Should any New Millennium customer think they've had a rough deal from BBC Customer Service, then they ain't seen nothing yet.

NUTTERS, NUMBSKULLS & GERIATRIC FASCISTS

'Dear viewer, you're a nutter says the BBC' headlined the *Daily Mail* as the first year of the New Millennium drew to a close. This revelation (allegedly) followed an otherwise simple request from a devoted Jean Simmons fan for the BBC to screen a season of her films. An equally avid autograph hunter to boot, the same licence payer also sought the Monika of BBC-1's new Controller. According to the *Mail* , not only did the BBC respond with what it described as a 'curt letter', but included with it was a Post-It note upon which was scribbled: 'Nutter, polite fob off – no autograph'.

Shocked and surprised, the 37-year-old nurse immediately winged the offending material directly to the desk of BBC's new director General, Greg Dyke (or 'Greg' as he prefers to be known in keeping with New BBC principles). Unfortunately, Greg did not respond personally. Instead a letter of apology was sent from 'The BBC' together with an invitation for the aggrieved correspondent and his wife to join the coach loads of others who weekly watch BBC shows being recorded. The

95

story was then sent to a doubtless gleeful *Daily Mail* Showbusiness Reporter. An unfortunate incident or a funny one, depending on whichever way you care to look at it. Such incidents will happen once in a while across millions of points of contact in any one year. Despite all the worship at the shrine of Customer Service, Auntie will always at some time be perceived as 'not giving a Tonbridge Toss' for the wants and desires of its licence payers.

John Reith was not only the founding father of the BBC, but its Customer Care ethic as well. He started the ball rolling in the early 1920s when he decided to reply personally to each and every 'discontented of Dagenham' less than thrilled with the results of twiddling a cat's whisker. The object of the exercise as he saw it was to satisfy as far as possible the near-infinite expectations of the licence payer. That across seven and a half subsequent decades BBC viewers and listeners were to be categorized, castigated and condemned would not have greatly surprised him.

'Vast as is the number of our correspondents", wrote Reith, "the inarticulate portion of the audience is infinitely greater than the articulate'. He found the contents of the BBC post-bag to be both 'interesting and highly instructive' and not 'without some element of amusement'. While he publicly welcomed the tidal wave of advice and criticism readily metered out by his subscribers, he soon began to question the value of his initiative.

'Periodically, letters come in,' he reflected, 'one per thousand or two, which make one doubt the sanity of the correspondent – in fact, there is little room for anything other than doubt.' The more his assessment continues, the more apparent it becomes that the BBC's post-bag had in fact become a box. Not unlike the one opened by a certain Pandora, and with a similarly troublesome lid. In many cases any attempt to satisfy was thwarted by an individual's personal and persistent worldview, revealing beneath Reith's otherwise austere, almost tyrannical facade, something of an innocent abroad.

It is clear that he was often quite shaken not only by their great expectations, but by the behaviour of some of this new breed of salvationist - The Listener. Unlike newspaper editors, long used to the foibles of allowing 'The Public' access via the Letters page, the top man at the BBC was much less case hardened. 'The situation is very peculiar', he wrote, freely admitting his lack of experience, that 'too much of it might induce considerable disgust with one's fellow creatures'. This was to remain a popular notion at the top level of BBC management for decades to come.

Those who deal directly with 'the public' these days do so blessed with professional training to industry standards defined by recognised 'Customer Service' best practice. This new breed is less easily shocked or surprised, even though the motives and tactics of Reith's more awkward customers remain the same.

Like those who despite best endeavours to cajole, placate and appease, remain stubbornly determined never to be satisfied. 'If the programme staff had been thorough blackguards,' lamented Reith, 'the virulence and vituperation conveyed by some of these rare communications could not have been increased'.

Every armchair critic in the land knows best how to run the BBC and what 'The Public' expects of it. Even back in 1924, such self-appointed watchdogs considered themselves to be the only soldiers in step as the parade passed by. Instead of accepting this, Reith looked longingly to the vast, silent majority who rarely, if ever, felt the need to forward their views. While he firmly believed that the BBC had a solemn duty to take seriously the views and opinions of those who financed it, he also recognised a responsibility on the part of the critic to be aware of the bigger picture.

Whether or not Reith wore the right size customer care hat all of the time is beside the point. Often his pronouncements are quite deliciously out of step in these more politically correct climes. Imagine today's Director General being as forthright in the BBC's Annual Report and Accounts. Sensibly, in 1924, Reith established a department dedicated to dealing with the BBC's huge post-bag. It was the Programme Correspondence Section that began to promote perceptions of BBC Customers.

The first list was drawn up in the BBC Handbook for 1928:

The Incorrigibles

This 'very curious type of critic' was on a par with today's domestic technocrats who purchase the very latest high-tech equipment only to enhance their capacity to highlight the shortcomings of whatever is broadcast. While the equipment has moved on in leaps and bounds, the driving force of the 'Incorrigible' has not. He was described as 'a most regular listener and delivers himself at frequent intervals of letters in which he points out that the BBC is, beyond doubt, a hotbed of incompetence and drivel. It is not quite certain whether such listeners derive pleasure or pain from their reception and correspondence.'

Latter day 'Incorrigibles' will have been amongst the first to buy Nicam stereo television sets in an area where that facility was not yet available. Or they rank amongst the first to own digital widescreen sets only to be thoroughly disgusted to discover not every programme is broadcast in that format. Even those programmes that are, never match the standards of those from 'the good old analogue days'.

The Martyrs

Of whom, 'a terrible mental picture is formed.' These comprised 'the foot-stamping variety that hope (in vain) that their pain and suffering will be sufficient to rock the BBC to its very foundations'.

The Anonymous Critic

'Minimum space was devoted' to those who would scribble: "Your programmes are ROTTEN on a postcard furtively dropped in a letter box round the next corner but one'. This type was not taken seriously, as they were considered 'so shockingly wasteful of time, stationery and postage!'

*

The highly refined bunch of 'gals' operating the Telephone Enquiry Bureau in the 1930s went only so far as to mention 'typical, choleric loud-voiced' persons. These required speaking to 'quietly'; so quietly and calmly that they would appreciate the difference and feel rather ashamed of themselves. Whereas, 'we must deal with telephone enquiries', stormed Lime Grove's irascible Chief Television Liaison Officer in the 1950s. 'For goodness sake', he banged on mercilessly, 'why must they ring? Why can't they let us get on with our job of putting programmes on the air?' Whilst accepting that it was part of a public service to give 'genuine information to sensible enquiries', there were those callers in need of good all round condemnation:

100

The Telephone Enquirer

This 'type' could have done much more to help the BBC. 'Sometimes they do not even trouble to dial the number, but simply demand that the GPO puts them through to the BBC'. When 'tempted to lift the phone' such callers failed to realize 'that the greater cost of that call would be born by the BBC'. Their call 'will monopolise one of the badly needed BBC phone lines. It will take up the time of one of the over-worked switchboard girls.' Further, 'if every producer, artist or announcer were to talk to even one caller in a hundred, programmes would be halted or even stopped!' Remember – 'Calls cost Time!'

The Telephone Commentator

Those 'who really have to register an opinion' should do so when the programme had finished. Or better still, wait until normal office hours the next day. 'We ask viewers NOT to telephone while the programme is on, but to wait until afterwards…but not PLEASE, not late at night!' Ringing the BBC had no effect in any case. Even if the BBC was physically able to accept ten thousand telephone calls on a single programme, it would be no real guide as to the opinion of many millions of others. Besides, the BBC already had its own listener and viewer research panels. These were 'the only reliable barometers of public opinion'. The only real effect resulting from 'allowing' such viewers to ring in was for them to 'let off steam.'

The Just for a Bet Brigade

'It is irritating for the BBC to be told often fifty or a hundred times a day, "I'm just ringing up to ask you something about the programme last night. It's to settle a wager"…'. This was intolerable. 'Such thoughtless and selfish numbskulls' calling only to settle a private bet were 'guilty of wasting BBC time'.

*

'Fortunately' (for him) long years in the business had left Lime Grove's Chief Liaison Officer 'case-hardened against telephone cranks.' Curiously, his attitude was not unlike that of Reith's, in that both men subscribed to the public service ethic and both were frustrated by its demands.

Maybe it was something to do with the swinging sixties, but hereafter BBC attitudes most definitely change. The world's largest television factory had opened in the form of Television Centre and on the fifth floor of the 'concrete doughnut' the Television Duty Office was established. Here, the obvious stresses and strains of Lime Grove were replaced by a new breed of carers intent on soothing and placating callers, making sure that they were received 'with gratitude and appreciation and their opinions respected.' Instead of perceiving callers as a nuisance, the new team of Television Duty Officers was now resolved to patronise them more as mildly errant offspring. The team did not wish to be regarded as 'mere officials' but more, as 'mothers' and 'nursemaids'. However, that curious preponderance to categorise callers remained.

The Knockers and Shockers
These 'specialised' in bias, prejudice, blasphemy and bad taste.

They were the most easily alarmed and quick to complain. 'So quick', that most of them ring up half-way through a programme without waiting to see whether their grievance will be put right.'

The Judicious Praisers

These were the careful and cautious ones, 'slow to anger, and also slow to dial.' They were reckoned to be more considerate than the Knockers and Shockers as they would wait at least fifteen minutes until after the programme had finished before they rang. This allowed them to fully consider their convictions. They tended to 'ring up with a precise, analytical statement of what they considered to have been good viewing.'

The Lonely Hearts

Mainly the elderly or those who lived alone, this 'sort' had 'no real inclination to discuss the merits of programmes'; rather they turned to the BBC as means of communicating with the outside world.

The Happy Chatters

Like the Lonely Hearts, they would ring up only wanting to talk about their own problems. They tended to call regularly after the same programme in the hope of speaking to their favourite duty officer.

The Lunatic Fringe

These were 'the nutty ones', a bunch of unfortunates credited as being 'the oddest of them all'. They would ring up about anything. They liked to have their say along with the sound of their own voices. 'And they ensure we hear them too, whether we like it or not'. They tended to surface according to the effects of lunar activity. In fact, periods of full moon activity were clearly marked on all duty office calendars. The 'many different kinds of lunacy' included the man who wanted to know the name of the Eiffel Tower, or the worried housewife whose husband was on the train to Birmingham. He had left his briefcase with all his paperwork at home. 'Can you relay a message to him', pleaded his wife, 'as he always listens to the radio in his car'.

'WHY MUST THEY RING?'

To try and encapsulate in one book, let alone in one chapter, all the reasons why viewers and listeners call and write to the BBC is an impossible task. Many have felt the frustrations endured by Lime Grove's choleric Chief Liaison Officer. But it's never a simple matter of wondering, 'why must they ring' rather, why the BBC prompts them to do so. That understood, it is possible to equip even the greenest recruit to the coalface with at least an idea of the great expectations ahead.

Viewers especially expect to see what they expect to see when they expect to see it. Lovers of sport expect BBC coverage to be uninterrupted and unadulterated by commentary; punditry or the expectations and interests of all others. The Licence Payer expects the BBC at all times to be impartial and unbiased (subject to their own opinions). When reporting war the British people expect the BBC to inform – not to educate or to entertain. The BBC is required at all times to remember that it is the British Broadcasting Corporation.

Opinion formers maintain there is too much sex and violence on television, while others want to know where it is. Repeat programmes are fine, provided viewers haven't seen them before. Everything was always so much better in the past. Whatever you want to know, Auntie must have made a programme about it; must be doing so, or must be about to. Thus it is possible to assemble a Top Ten of perennial blunders and bloomers; misjudgments and misunderstandings, each guaranteed to light up the switchboard and bust the gut of the postman:

• Re-scheduling

Re-scheduling is the single largest contaminate responsible for ruining even the best-laid plans. It is the kindling that fuels the fire of discontent amongst the multitude more than any other issue. Its virulence is further magnified by an ability to confuse what is perceived to be a scheduling matter with an altogether different beast. Scheduling is the art of placing programmes at specific times; re-scheduling is about disrupting, decimating or destroying them.

Re-scheduling comes about due to circumstances either beyond or in the control of broadcasters. The BBC particularly is required – indeed expected - to respond to the issues of the day, whether that be (God forbid) a train crash or the death of a world leader. Here a scheduled programme might be deemed

108

to be in bad taste in which case it will be removed and replaced with another. News programmes may be extended or special programming replacing the ones in the advertised schedule.

At the time of writing, with only two terrestrial television channels that are required to complement each other to provide choice, this remains a conundrum. Re-scheduling this delicate balance can and does alienate huge sections of the audience. But now there is digital broadcasting and with it hundreds of channels to choose from. For those that have access, a little red button allows for everyone to become a couch scheduler. If you want to watch the News or sport or even old quiz shows all day long you can now do so. But until such time as we all have to go digital, BBC-1 and BBC-2 will still have to cope with satisfying the needs of everyone all of the time.

When it comes to the dropping of scheduled programmes, there is little by way of comfort that can be extended except to remind viewers that programmes are invariably repeated. Which creates another thorny issue. Then there are those scheduled programmes that just disappear without warning. *The Cumbrian Tales* mystery is a classic example. This was a series about life in a typical Cumbrian village proving quite popular within the new vogue for fly-on-the-wall 'docu-soaps'. So it came as something of a shock for viewers to find one week it was there and the next week it was gone.

An on-air announcement attempted to explain that a particular element of the series went against the BBC's Producers' Guidelines. These are the rules and regulations governing the behaviour of programme makers. Included is the matter of probity wherein the programme makers must not benefit from any vested commercial interest in their programmes. As it happened the series producer owned the village pub, which was heavily featured throughout. But viewers mostly couldn't understand these 'weird BBC constraints'. They were enjoying the series, wanted to continue enjoying it and so complained accordingly about its 'arbitrary removal'.

Re-scheduling in its purest form affects that which is advertised to be on air at a specific date and time but which, for whatever reason, is not. Cult and Sci-Fi fans are not shy in coming forward to vent their collective spleen when their programmes are dropped. This section of the audience is only narrowly beaten by sports fans when it comes to complaints about how "ill-served" they are by the BBC. Mix the two together and you have an explosive combination. While sports fans expect the BBC to maintain live coverage until the bitter end, 'Trekkies' especially go ape when the last over at Lords vapourises their programme from the schedule, or a tie-break at Wimbledon conspires to castrate Captain Kirk. Once, even a government White Paper on the future of the BBC was drawn into the Sci-

Fi fray. In it was contained the recommendation for a greater responsiveness to the needs of the licence payer. This resulted in hundreds of *Doctor Who* fans taking the opportunity to urge the BBC 'to make a start' by returning the series to the screen.

Affording due coverage to breaking national and international stories is as much expected of the BBC as the consequences can be condemned. Of the host of disasters and horror stories over the years, the sinking of the Zeebrugge car ferry and Hillsborough come readily to mind. As do the events of Sunday August 31 1997. The airwaves throughout that bleak Bank Holiday Sunday were occupied with little else. The tragic events of the previous night gave way to the story slowly unfolding throughout the day and late into the evening when the body of Diana, Princess of Wales was brought home.

The Television Information Office logged in excess of 6,000 calls. Most of these were complaints about excessive or simultaneous coverage on BBC-1 and 2 or the subsequent disruption to published schedules. The following Saturday, coverage of the funeral netted a further 3000 calls, but the number of complaints was negligible. Possibly, given the emotions of the week and the atmosphere of that day, even the most ardent critics for once selflessly let their observations drop.

The Antiques Roadshow was suddenly and unceremoniously dropped mid-way for live coverage of the release of Nelson Mandela. This 'appalling act' (on the part of the BBC) resulted in over 500 calls of 'disgust and outrage'. It was deemed intolerable that this 'Sunday institution' should be so slighted in favour of a 'convicted terrorist's release from gaol'. People all over the globe were bearing witness to history in the making. Millions watched live one man's walk to freedom signal the life-change of an entire nation. But this was as nothing compared to the loss of Hugh Scully and chums pricing Aunt Nellie's teapot. It was a rude interruption to the advertised schedule. It was not supposed to happen. It was not expected and should therefore not have occurred. Full stop. End of story.

The committed scheduphile is no respecter of seasonal goodwill. Even at Christmas the spectre of schedule changes can rear its ugly head more times than Marley's ghost to make a mockery of the bumper edition of *Radio Times*. Changes to the advertised schedule are bad enough at other times of the year but at Christmas it's far worse when the single biggest source of home entertainment is the box. Here scheduling changes are about as welcome as a strike by Santa's workforce. That said, these inconveniences are not always the fault of broadcasters or programme guides. Like the woman who failed to appreciate the reason why she was unable to watch *Delia Smith* 'as advertised'. This was because she was going by a copy of *Radio*

Times some two weeks out of date. Nevertheless it was still somehow the fault of the BBC and required the registering of the 'strongest possible complaint.'

Or the woman who complained that not all radio drama was restricted to 90 minutes. Her anger centered on a play called *Ways of Escape* that had exceeded this time. So good was the play that she had been unable to tear herself away from the radio. The BBC had therefore been responsible for her nearly missing her flight to a little winter sun. Oddest of all was the man who claimed to have spent the festive period with the late film star, Steve McQueen. He claimed he had been "forced to apologise on behalf of the nation" for the lack of The Great Escape in the schedules, "now as much a part of Christmas as nuts and crackers". Enough said.

Not even armed conflict involving British troops escapes the attention of the scheduphile. Large numbers of licence payers complained about the disruption to schedules resulting from the Falklands War. Radio 4 FM netted over 1,000 calls of complaint about 'saturation coverage' disrupting regular programmes. This was despite Radio 4 Long Wave providing an alternative service in order to preserve as much of the regular schedule as possible. But this was of little comfort to those listeners unable to receive acceptable reception on Long Wave. One such frustrated would-be listener rang from her garden.

She claimed to have spent the entire afternoon waving around a wire coathanger attached to her radio without success. It was suggested that she re-tune to Radio 4 FM for a better reception. At which point she declared: "What's the use of FM to me? I've only got one eye!"

National and international disasters, major or world events aside, one strain of the re-scheduling virus exists that is particularly virulent. And that comes in the form of sport. Once upon a time the BBC enjoyed an immense and varied portfolio of sports coverage. For the most part it was crammed into either the Saturday or Sunday *Grandstand* schedule. The strains of that familiar forty-year old theme tune still heralds the prospect of hours of sport to come. Except that in the New Millennium the range and variety is far less than it once was.

With so many contracts at the BBC's disposal, sporting dates or timings (or both) would quite often clash. This was known in advance of course and the allocated transmission times duly published. But moments of special excitement still result in sticking with whatever is proving to be so at the time. Not that long ago, both BBC channels could be blocked off for sport from midday to early evening. ITV would be airing its own sports magazine at the same time, with Channel 4 screening a Serbo-Croat movie with subtitles (before they won the Racing contract, that is).

Where it is known in advance that there is likely to be disruption to the planned schedule, action can be taken to try to avoid disappointment. The provision of alternative schedules for the final stages of World Cup football is one example. The idea here is to try to make it clear what will be shown in the event of say, a British team getting through to the quarter finals, and where the BBC has secured the broadcast rights. Because it cannot be known in advance what will be the state of play on publication of *Radio Times*, the schedules on the days in question will be split into two.

'Pattern A' might show the regular schedule and 'Pattern B' the proposed schedule if it was decided to cover, say, a quarter final game. So, up to ten days in advance of transmission, viewers are informed in print and sometimes on-air, what they can expect on which channel, at what time, or whichever evening, according to whatever circumstances. And for the most part, it works. But not always. If 'Pattern A' is transmitted, there will inevitably be those complaining that they are unable to receive their preferred 'Pattern B'.

There should be marketed something called 'The Scheduling Game' to emulate the rigours of controlling a broadcasting company. Each player is given a remit of running either a public, an entertainment or an information based service. Complete with a budget, each 'station' would then bid for the range of programmes on offer. These programmes would have to fill a schedule with appropriate material that would satisfy both the audience as well as the broadcasters' share of the market. The Commercial players would need to appease advertisers or sponsors and the public service providers to justify a licence fee. Both would have to please all of the people all of the time. Just imagine the scope for increased family rows, with endless recriminations about who wants to watch what, when and why.

November 16th 1993 is a date lodged in scheduling decision-making infamy. This was when a BBC executive was named as the man 'who sparked off a record protest from viewers'. *The Times* newspaper claimed that 'more than 20,000 viewers jammed the BBC switchboard' as a result of 'easily the most difficult decision' a sports Editor had ever had to make. It was the final round of qualification games for the 1994 World Cup. England and Wales both had a chance to qualify but England had to win by 10 goals in San Marino and hope that Holland were beaten by Poland. Wales had to beat Romania in Cardiff. The Editor's dilemma was that both games were being played at the same time with only one channel at his disposal. In his later confessional, the Editor described how he spent the previous week deliberating with himself about which game to show.

To take England off the air in England would be, he knew, nothing short of heresy. He knew that such a move would light up the duty log 'like a Christmas tree.' Hour after hour he went through the permutations. When would it be safe to leave the England game and under what circumstances? Within 15 minutes on the day, with the most remarkable opening to an

England International in football history, San Marino was ahead. England was sluggish to say the least but more importantly, the Dutch were beating Poland and it was looking therefore highly unlikely that England would qualify. In fact it was looking extremely unlikely. Then Wales got a penalty. It was crunch time.

The Editor shouted to John Motson (doubtless along with 90 per cent of the audience) who was commentating on the England game: 'Shut up Motty, we're going to Wales'. At that moment, Wales were setting up for the penalty. It would indeed take a brave man (or a foolhardy one) to take a live England international off the air in England. But that's exactly what this Editor did; transferring to coverage from Cardiff. Wales missed the penalty. It was getting very tight and they still needed one goal to qualify for the World Cup. England still needed a very big miracle. Having gone across to Wales, the Editor had to stay there. Meanwhile, horror upon horror, while viewers watched Wales lose 2-1, England had netted three goals in 10 short minutes and went on to win 7-1.

In the end neither team qualified. It goes without saying what the reaction was from England fans. A seething 700 of them demanded to know who had made the decision and why. The 'who' bit was easy. It was the why bit that everyone else had more difficulty with. The press too was in hot pursuit. According to the Editor, an estimated 20,000 calls had poured into the duty log, adding, almost boastfully, 'the highest number they had ever had'. He then informed *Times* readers how he later went over and over his actions. Had he made the right decision or had he simply gambled on breaking a golden rule, and lost? Apparently all and sundry were telling him that he was right. As their boss they were unlikely to say otherwise.

The episode occupied the front page of *The Times* (a copy of which hangs in the offending Editor's bathroom). Was he brave or foolhardy? Probably a bit of both, he reckoned. Whatever, he looked upon it as 'a great escape'. He genuinely believed he had made the right decision. His reputation had been put through the shredder by the press but he 'escaped' with his career intact. 'England didn't escape because they didn't qualify', he concluded, 'but I reckon I did because I went to the USA to edit the BBC's coverage of the World Cup.'

But then, think about it. Putting to one side all the issues arising before, during and after the game, and given all the permutations, what would you have done? Just for a moment put yourself in that Editor's shoes. What if Wales had qualified and England had been slaughtered? What then? It is easy with the benefit of hindsight. But at the time someone has to make a decision, and that they don't come much tougher than that.

• Sport

A newspaper columnist once expressed the view that people are 'bigoted and vituperative when they talk about their politics, but informed and lucid when they talk about their sport.' This is a view not necessarily supported by the duty logs, at least as far as sport is concerned. Coverage of one FA Cup Final had been as predictable as ever. Viewers in Scotland bemoaned the fact they were unable to see it – even though the rights to the English Cup Final do not extend to Scotland. Commentators were all biased, or blind, or both. And the cameras always cut away just as the band started to play at half-time, 'which', according to one viewer, 'is what most people really want to see'.

Of the 182 complaints received, the majority included the obligatory abuse of studio pundits. 'Why do we have to listen to Jimmy Hill?'; 'Jimmy Hill is an idiot'; 'he's well past his best'; 'he hasn't got a clue, he should be pensioned off'; 'I would like Jimmy Hill's money to sit there and talk such utter rubbish' etc., etc. John Motson was (as ever) variously accused of ruining 'every game of football with his drivel'; ' he talks a load of rubbish'….. 'please get him to shut up'. He was also accused of being 'very patronising to short people', following his continual references to the diminutive stature of the Chelsea players. Alan Hansen got off comparatively scot-free (no pun intended). Just one caller phoned in to say that he was "hopelessly inept."

In the year 2001 it is difficult to believe that less than eight FA Cup Finals ago, sport, especially on weekends used to guarantee bumper editions of the duty Log. Once, not that long ago, thousands upon thousands of sports fans and non-fans alike complained year in and year out about the sporting events that were or were not shown; the sheer amount of them, the lack of them, or any alternative to them. Since 1992, with the loss to Sky television of the rights to show Premier League football, both the BBC and ITV have gradually been drained of their sporting duopoly. Curiously however, this erosion of sport from the BBC menu did not lead to a massive uprising from licence-fee payers. In fact, for the most part it had quite the reverse effect. Towards the end of the 90s it was becoming rare for the

121

Television Log to bulge with sport-related issues. Whereas Auntie might have lost her football, her cricket, her boxing, her England rugby etc., she still had the Boat Race, Ascot, The Grand National and of course, Wimbledon.

The BBC first began covering Wimbledon tennis on the radio in 1927. Exactly 10 years later the first television broadcasts began. Since the advent in 1964 of BBC-2, viewers have enjoyed a double helping of the annual lawn tennis championships along with their strawberries and cream. In all, some 35 televised years of rain-dashed hopes for a British champion. Bags of time, you would think, for avid TV fans to predict with a high degree of accuracy the foibles of BBC coverage. Few complainers nowadays have reason to castigate politically incorrect commentators calling female players 'girls', when they are obviously grown women. But the BBC is still roundly condemned for curtailing coverage at a crucial point. Such as too much attention afforded even the most hapless British hopeful when a more popular player is in action elsewhere. Or too little attention paid to the hapless British hopeful.

There will always be those who feel that there is altogether too much coverage of Wimbledon, and those who believe there's too little. Until we all turn digital, there will remain legions who object to 'having to suffer' coverage on both BBC-1 and BBC-2.

In all probability with its own digital channel devoted to it, the question of 'the BBC's fascination with Centre Court when there are better games going on elsewhere' will no longer arise. Likewise the showing of Court One when there is prime action on Centre Court. Or showing the Outside Courts when the BBC should be concentrating on Centre court. And Court One.

When rain stops play, the replays of previous games are never the ones 'everyone' wants to see. Some want to see the bits 'everyone' missed earlier in the day when they were at work. Others claim that 'everyone' would much prefer to watch what they consider to be 'classic' matches of the past. Then there are those who are sure that 'everyone' is 'sick of being forced to watch this rubbish' and would much prefer a cartoon instead. And, last but not least, there is the grand old chestnut of them all: the continuity break.

This particular feature will blossom annually for as long as BBC-1 and BBC-2 continue to cover live Wimbledon tennis. At ten past four each weekday afternoon, BBC-1 gives way to Children's programmes and BBC-2 takes over coverage. For less than two-minutes there is the same picture on both channels. This is known as the continuity break. It ensures that viewers can switch channels without missing a second of the action. It harps back to the days before the remote, when you had to get out of the armchair to manually switch channels. But no matter what the reason, the telephones will instantly become red hot with demands to know: 'why are you showing the same game on both channels?' Every year the same explanation is patiently afforded the affronted. It's almost as if some of them wait until exactly ten minutes past four to channel hop. Often, before they've ploughed through their complaint, the source of their grievance has become history.

As demonstrated earlier in the Scheduling section, only Russian Roulette comes close to a Sports Editor's decision to switch to another game. And here, Wimbledon is certainly no stranger to this risky business. But in 1993 we were not talking about just any old game. Among the deluge of callers going ballistic then was journalist Lynn Barber. In her subsequent piece for the *Independent on Sunday*, she made plain the experience of one household having their expectations dashed by BBC Television. She began by correcting the claims of other papers that the BBC switchboard was 'jammed' on the evening in question. As she learned later, such a phenomenon is not technically possible. The switchboard had in reality been 'heavily engaged'. In fact it had been engaged for many hours. Not – as other papers had claimed because Pete Sampras had used bad language on court - but for a reason far worse than that, as Ms Barber could attest to as one of the people 'doing the jamming'.

At 6.25pm on that fateful Monday evening, seemingly every Wimbledon fanatic in the land was deeply engrossed in Andre Agassi's gripping match against Krajicek. Then the commentator announced that 'we are going over to Court 14' to watch British hopeful Andrew Foster's match against Pete Sampras. 'You cannot be serious!' exclaimed Ms Barber in harmony with millions of other flabbergasted viewers. There was no competition (let alone any interest) in watching even a British hopeful when Andre Agassi was in full flight. So like thousands of others, Lynn Barber did that which she had never done before in her life and rang the BBC to complain.

At least she tried to, but because of the sheer ferocity of feeling from an entire nation venting its spleen on the perpetrator of this dastardly act, it took her a full 67 minutes to even get through to the main switchboard. When she finally hitched a ride on the Information Office's new call queuing system, she had to wait another five minutes 'listening to a tape-recorded message saying that I was being held in a call queuing system.' When she eventually got through she was listened to 'courteously' as she demanded to know when her screen would again be blessed with Agassi and why was he taken off in the first place?

The reason was of course that the Editor had decided to cover 'the British interest'. Offering as much to such patently furious callers would have gone down like the Titanic. An assurance was given that the complaint would be logged. Which was little consolation. Even more galling was in the time that it had taken to register the complaint, Agassi had fought two sets to tie-break and Foster had been comprehensively trounced by Sampras. So it was the very next day that Ms Barber called the BBC in journalistic mode to ask whether her experience as a complainant was typical. It was not, she was told. That night was bad. Not unusually bad. Not as bad as when *Casualty* accounted for 48 hours of non-stop complaints. In all 215 grievances were logged about the Agassi match – or rather the lack of it. But even so, amidst this minor catastrophe, there

126

were lighter moments. Such as the old lady who got through in the middle of it all to ask for information about "the Dead Sea Squirrels" she had seen on a past *Chronicle* programme.

Where football once topped the league of perceived sport surfeit, hot on its heels by the early 80s came the World Snooker Championships. Together, these two heavyweights could and would decimate published schedules at the drop of a hat. Darts too could score a treble-bull with as many as 300 complaints a throw, whereas sometimes attempts not to disrupt advertised programmes could net just as many. Fans of Bowls (of which there are a great many) were once outraged when a tournament was taken off at a crucial stage in order to keep to the schedule. Such a decision would not have been made during a football match, a snooker or darts tournament or a cricket match, or any other sport at such a stage, so why Bowls it was asked? A good question, but with no real answer as coverage was terminated to show of all things a repeat *Horizon* documentary that could have been shown any time.

When dealing with the subject of sporting expectations, credibility can be stretched to the limit. Royal Ascot was spoiled for one viewer by 'the continual showing of unimportant and insignificant horse races'. These were 'ruining enjoyment of the fashion display, which is, after all, the purpose of Royal Ascot.'

127

Another viewer once complained that Frank Bruno's treatment of Jose Ribalta in the ring was "no way to treat a visitor to these shores". It is not unreasonable to expect sports presenters, commentators and pundits to present, commentate or opine, for that is what they are paid to do. However one the longest running hardy perennials listed in the BBC complaints catalogue is the plea for them all to shut up. Des Lynam aside, most presenters, commentators and pundits play to an audience whose personal knowledge of sport far outweighs 'those twits on TV'. One woman for example complained that her husband had been 'forced to go and lie down', as he was 'beginning to agree with Jimmy Hill'.

• **Bias**

Bias as a complaint category is by no means a big one, but sufficient to vex BBC sensibilities. It is on the political front where incidences of bias are best spotted or demonstrated, if not easily understood. There was once a debate on *Panorama*, when a panel of journalists questioned the three Labour leadership candidates for the Euro elections. The *Daily Mail*'s Ann Leslie stood accused of asking questions that allowed the politicians to present themselves in the best possible light. Which was most odd, given the *Mail*'s political leaning. But the viewers had spoken. Unless care is taken, the use of fresh as against canned tomatoes in cookery programmes, cars shown on *Top*

Gear or the choice of bands featured on *Top of the Pops* can all be assigned to the Bias category. A screening of the feature film *Khartoum* once led to an allegation that 'the BBC was biased against Arabs', and the showing of cricket highlights after 11pm was seen by one viewer as 'further evidence of the BBC's bias against the existence of God'.

Here Is The News was an inventive series of mock BBC Television News programmes marking the 50th anniversary of the outbreak of World War Two. It was produced in the style of contemporary News formats with Sue Lawley 'reading the news' complete with 1940s make up and clothes that she might well prefer to forget. The idea was to report the actual events across the weeks leading up to the outbreak of war. As a lead-in to the BBC's 50th Anniversary package, the intention should have been clear to everyone, and for the most part it was. Except for the one viewer who complained of 'anti-German bias.'

A technical failure resulted in the loss of a live link-up with Dame Vera Lynn and Bob Hope aboard the QE2. A filler programme had to be found quickly to occupy the otherwise blank screens. But one featuring 'squirrels shagging' was not considered the most appropriate substitute. When a recording of the ill-fated duet was shown the following week, hundreds complained about the 'abysmal quality and content' of the show, which led one viewer to suggest that 'everyone at the BBC was biased against the war dead.' Only the BBC would take the time and trouble to categorise such original perceptions. These few examples fall into the BBC's Bias category only because the caller or correspondent has uttered the noun. They clearly demonstrate something of a grey area. Unlike that Big Daddy of them all with all its attendant mischiefs: Political Bias.

The Party Conferences used to produce a healthy batch of confirmed bias sightings. At these annual events, a huge amount of care and attention is paid in ensuring that all three Parties enjoy proportional airtime. Also that the big issues are covered, questioned and challenged, and that the major speeches are captured as far and as equitably as is possible. But this can count for little. No sooner can these conferences be under way than storms of protest will follow any interruption to a speech (no matter how long) or comments made by (biased) commentators. No Tory will ever agree that their Party enjoyed the same treatment as did Labour. And vice versa. No Liberal Democrat would agree that their coverage was proportional to that of Labour or the Tories.

Balance as far as broadcasting is concerned is something struck over time. But this cuts little ice when it comes to political bias. 'Anyway, it is well-known that you BBC people are all a bunch of bright Red Tory Pinkos!' stated one caller on the Radio Log in 1975. That comment could have been logged half an hour

ago and might well be in an hour's time or ten years from now. BBC-2's news spoof *The Day Today* attracted one call demanding to know 'which left-wing pinkie Trot' was responsible for including a sketch showing John Major punching the Queen.

For as long as there has been a BBC there has been friction between it and the government of the day, and it's as well to remember that. The British Broadcasting Company was not a public corporation when the General Strike came about in 1926.

The BBC came very close to being taken over by those who thought like Winston Churchill that the Company should become an arm of the government. As it happened the Prime Minister, Stanley Baldwin, did not want that to happen although he expected of the BBC not to broadcast anything likely to damage the position of the government. Even though Reith couldn't offer those sympathetic to the strike the same facilities he was obliged to offer the government, the public was generally happy with the service provided. All in all it was mostly agreed that the BBC was a significant factor in holding the country together during the crisis. The rest, as they say, is history. Forty odd years later, the BBC fell equally foul of Harold Wilson and his Labour government, and later still with the Conservative administration under Margaret Thatcher.

Thatcherite policy included an end to what was perceived as the ambiguity of the BBC's place in the broadcasting industry. It was time to end the licence fee and to see the BBC, or at least parts of it privatised. For over a decade, extreme pressure was placed on the corporation to change or suffer the consequences. No opportunity was lost to find sufficiently damaging material with which to beat the BBC. Day by day the pages of the Duty Logs sizzled with the tang of left-wing bias or examples of low moral content in programmes. Conservative Party Central Office was highly effective in marshalling supporters and activists to keep up the pressure. Sometimes however it was a naturally occurring process. At the height of the 1987 General Election, a series of live phone-programmes called *On The Spot* went out on BBC-1 prime-time.

The Tories were no fans of such a format; nor its presenter, Sue Lawley. For still raw in the memory was Mrs Thatcher's ill-fated appearance on a *Nationwide Special* prior to the 1983 General Election. This too was hosted by Sue Lawley and included live calls from viewers. One of the questions put to the Prime Minister came from a schoolteacher concerned about the sinking of the Argentine warship General Belgrano during the Falklands War. Soon into the intercourse the caller was clearly dissatisfied with the lack of a clear answer given by the Prime Minister. Mrs Thatcher too was by now becoming increasingly restless. Instead of moving rapidly on to the next question as the Prime Minister was clearly hoping, the conflict was allowed to continue. The Iron Lady had met her match and was roundly humiliated live in front of millions. Inevitably, large numbers of viewers began condemning the BBC for giving Labour leader, Neil Kinnock, a soft-ride by comparison.

It was as presenter of *On The Spot* that Sue Lawley once again found herself in hot water. According to the *Daily Mail* she 'tried to rough up' the Tory party chairman, Norman Tebbit. The idea of anyone – let alone Sue Lawley - 'roughing up' Norman Tebbit, is a bit like imagining Julian Clarey attempting likewise in the ring with Mike Tyson. Norman Tebbit was more than capable of holding his own against any media pundit. Nevertheless, the *Mail* dutifully sailed to his defence with all guns blazing. According to 'hundreds of viewers' the 'TV girl' continually interrupted 'in a steady stream of hostile reactions'. And the Tory chairman was not alone in facing unbridled BBC hostility that same evening. The *Mail* discovered that some callers were treated 'equally as roughly' when they tried to complain.

One of the Viewers 'insulted' by the BBC in protest at the Tebbit phone-in, was a retired salesman from South East London. 'I thought the programme was highly biased against Mr Tebbit', the salesman told the *Mail*. He felt that Sue Lawley did not give Tebbit a chance to answer questions properly. When the retired salesman rang the BBC to complain he was kept waiting for some time. When he finally got through, 'the duty officer' listened to what he had to say before declaring: 'in any case the Conservatives do not stand a chance of winning'. Then, before the phone was 'rudely slammed down on him' the caller was told to 'Bugger off'.

Mr Tebbit refused to be drawn into the controversy himself. He insisted instead that *Daily Mail* readers should judge for themselves whether or not the BBC was biased. He urged them to complain directly to the BBC if they thought that the treatment metered out him was hostile, which of course they did in their droves. Partly out of this was created the variant: 'interviewing techniques', complete with its own set of fresh invectives such as 'intrusiveness' and 'aggressiveness'.

In 1991, the new Conservative Party Chairman (Chris Patton) made a call to conference to "watch carefully for political bias on radio and TV in the run-up to the General Election and to jam the switchboards of the guilty channels." Local constituencies were urged to set up broadcasting monitoring teams. To help them in this cause, Central Office would supply a full list of broadcasting organisations, their producers and editors – including addresses and phone numbers. To loud applause, Chris Patten said he knew that many members were deeply concerned about the incidence of bias "too often and understandably so." "So when you are angry," he urged, "phone them, above all phone them on the spot. If necessary, jam the switchboards." Broadcasters, he went on, had to realise that in a free society they were publicly accountable. He wasn't asking for a Conservative Broadcasting Corporation, merely the right to expect fair broadcasting 'in our democracy.'

Few would argue with that. And few did. If anything, the tactic backfired. Instead of doing as Mr Patten suggested, some of the party's staunchest supporters were appalled by the idea of such blatant political pressure being exerted on the BBC, from any quarter. Others meanwhile dutifully did as they were bid.

Some four months in advance of the General Election, Terry Wogan interviewed a guest from the Labour party on his chat show. This was condemned by hundreds of Tory supporters that it was wrong to have such a guest 'almost on the eve of the General Election'. Moreover, the BBC had the studio 'packed to the gunnels with 'Lefties'.

As the big day drew closer, 3,000 British Telecom subscribers had thought it good to balk. Over 800 claims of bias were spotted by the ever-vigilant supporters of the Conservative Party; Labour came a close second with 771, and the Liberal Democrats a poor third with a mere 57 confirmed sightings of bias. Even so, this didn't stop a rare Labour / Tory collective complaining that the Lib Dems were enjoying altogether far too much coverage. Yet another coalition, this time comprising Labour and Lib Dem supporters, added an imaginative edge to the proceedings in the joint discovery of a fresh incidence of pro-Tory bias. This came in the form of a blue backdrop to the *Election '92* studio, which was seen as a 'subliminal message' to voters. The fact that the colour blue happens to make technical studio wizardry work was of no interest. 'People associate that colour with the Tories,' one objection went, 'now they associate the BBC with them too. Shame on you all.'

Across any General Election, the audience reaction will always be the same. Each of the main Party leaders will be offered an airing - or a dressing down – according to whichever perception.

When interviewing (or interrogating) Party Leaders, the interviewers (or interrogators) will be 'far more rude and aggressive' with the Tory leader than they will be 'with the others'. All in all, however, the John Major years were less combative than they had been under Mrs Thatcher. It was interesting during the 2001 General Election to hear Prime Minister Tony Blair and his Deputy, John Prescott complain about 'the media staging stunts'. In reality, the public drubbing of Mr Blair by a highly disgruntled NHS user was not the stuff to stop News cameras rolling. Likewise Mr Prescott's left hook into the face of an egg-throwing heckler. There will always be the odd eruption between the government of the day and the BBC. Certain perceptions will remain unshakeable. Rankling politicians is part of the BBC's job – or should be. For the most part, most politicians realize this and relish the opportunity to openly cross swords with it.

• **War**

The Television Information Office Log for December 16 1998 reported 'a good day until the attack on Baghdad in the evening put paid to excellent statistics.' This neatly sums up changes in emphasis on the road towards BBC Customer Service. Previously the headlines would have centred on yet another armed conflict taking place. But at this moment in time in the history of the coalface, collateral damage to the statistics had become the key issue. The largest number of calls condemned the BBC for sleeping with the enemy. Pro-Iraqi bias complaints numbered 113, with less than 20 for pro-US bias. Aside from that there were less than 60 other calls mostly complaining about the termination of Westminster coverage earlier in the day, and four appreciations for doing so. In total less than 200 calls were logged. By midnight the lines were quiet and the office closed. The low number of calls and the impact on performance targets aside, this was typical of public reaction to the BBC's reporting of armed conflict involving British personnel.

Some months later, British forces formed part of the NATO initiative to try to call a halt to the horrors taking place in Kosova. Once again, the BBC "was guilty of giving away vital military intelligence". John Simpson reporting from Belgrade was deemed to be in the pay of the enemy propaganda machine, and the BBC's 'objectivity did not match the patriotic mood'. According to some, BBC coverage was little short of traitorous.

Lobby groups from both sides of the argument attempted to flood the Corporation with emails, letters and phone calls demanding to see aired their versions of events taking place in the former Yugoslavia. Not to show the full horror would have smacked of partiality or even censorship. Yet 'littering the screens with the awful scenes of barbarity' was putting many viewers off their evening meal.

In times of crisis the BBC becomes 'the nation's broadcaster'. Much of this perception was born of the part it played during World War Two. Its famous dot-dot-dot-dash 'V for Victory' call sign signalled the start of broadcasts to those countries under German and Italian occupation. The BBC also had a primary role to play on the home front. Entertainment was seen as the most effective means of boosting morale and countering German propaganda. But that was then and the world has since moved on.

Today, BBC audiences across all constituent factors are quite clear as to their expectations of the BBC in times of war. During The Gulf War, the Corporation was condemned for filling the screens with dramatic pictures, legions of studio experts and very little else. Presenter Peter Snow was particularly vilified for fronting his very own Theatre of War played out in a sandpit strewn with construction kit armour and polyfilla bunkers.

Altogether this smacked of the new 'infotainment' ideology and the audience didn't like it. The BBC felt there was a need to provide information even when there was none of any value. This is now all too familiar with rolling news, endlessly repeating the same information while anxiously awaiting a fresh snippet of breaking news.

The Falklands War saw much greater heavy political and public artillery aimed at both Broadcasting House and Television Centre. Worst hit was the latter due to a near total lack of live (and even recorded) pictures of what was happening. This led to a very public disagreement between the BBC, the Ministry of Defence and others. It was inconceivable that in the age of satellite technology, there was no live coverage of what was happening to British troops. Criticism would almost certainly have been softened if there had been at least some supportive footage of British action in the South Atlantic. Unfortunately all that was available was from the Argentines depicting the enemy point of view. Mrs Thatcher and her ministers openly accused the BBC of not presenting the British case, or more accurately that of her government.

Moreover, it was alleged that what information was available was giving away military secrets. Film coverage of a naval funeral in Argentina did not help matters and even John Cole, the BBC's Chief Political Editor, soon became the focus of suspicion. According to some licence payers, his distinct Ulster brogue 'openly displayed his nationality' and therefore his 'inherent treachery'. David Dimbleby managed to upset a large number of people following his 'rude and aggressive' interview with Defence Minister, John Nott, who, live on air, ripped off his microphone in disgust before storming out of the studio.

In reply to a related question in the House of Commons, Mrs Thatcher declared: "Our people are very robust and the heart of Britain is sound. I hope that every individual will make their views directly known to the BBC, by their letters and telephone calls". This they did. Over a six week period, close on 4,000 calls were logged of which 75% claimed that the BBC was biased in favour of the Argentines. Most of these callers had not seen the full range of BBC coverage for themselves, but were doing what 'The Leader (sic.)' recommended. Many just rang to yell: 'you traitor!' before slamming down the 'phone. Others enquired if they were through to 'The Argentine Broadcasting Corporation'.

The opening credits to *Panorama* or the *Nine o'clock News* had barely rolled before calls would come through demanding, 'get this treachery off my screen!!!'. A later survey showed the majority of these callers to be largely articulate, well-spoken; middle-aged, possibly with some experience of World War Two. Their motivation was based on patriotic reasons. It was this that 'might have led to some heated comments and emotional attitudes'. Even so, there were lighter moments, such as the call from a Miss Scales of Weybridge complaining of imbalance.

Four years later, the 'issuing of enemy propaganda' was topping the list of complaints about BBC coverage of The Gulf War.

This included any objective viewpoint or generalisation deemed to be sympathetic to the Iraqi cause. A prime example was Jeremy Bowen's report of stray allied bombing, which destroyed a civilian shelter in Baghdad. 'Probing questions of potential use to the enemy' was another hangover from the Falklands War. This was despite the fact that information came directly, and often on-screen, from the Ministry of Defence or commanders in the field. One caller likened the BBC's 'tactics' to those used by Hitler's radio stooge, Lord Haw Haw. And footage of British POWs was designed to undermine the resolve of 'our boys'. The 'hanging of a portrait of Saddam Hussein behind the newsreaders' deepened these suspicions. No sooner would a graphic of the Iraqi leader accompany a report than a shower of complaints would flood in to the 'Baghdad Broadcasting Company'.

As ever, no sooner did this conflict end than things quickly returned to normal. There were of course still those viewers and listeners 'suffering'. The woman from Surrey comes to mind. She demanded to know the exact time and date that the BBC transmitted pictures of troops returning home from The Gulf. There had been a number of such reports so her request was not as straightforward as she first thought. But this was all irrelevant to her; what she wanted was the time and the date. When pressed as to why she needed such precise information, she explained. It was the same day that next door's mongrel had got over her fence and ruined her pedigree poodle. The woman in question was at the time glued to the box – otherwise greater vigilance would have been maintained. She needed this information for her planned court appearance. Provided she was given the information she was prepared to overlook 'the BBC's participation in this matter'.

• Nationalism/Britishness

Extreme care must be taken by the BBC when using the words 'British' or 'English'. Huge numbers of complaints have been registered down the decades triggered by the use of British to describe things English, and English to describe things British. 'British football hooligans' is the classic example when used to more correctly describe England supporters. Conversely a 'British' win at, say the Olympics, by someone English and described as such will bring forth cries of foul play on behalf of the 'British' team effort.

In the 1940s the BBC Variety Programmes Guide contained strict guidance as to the correct use of 'British' and 'English'. Such guides were the arbiters of taste and decency governing what variety artistes could and could not say. Along with references to 'lavatories', 'fig leaves' and 'lodgers', rules regarding the use of 'British' and 'English' were quite clear: 'The mis-use of the word English, where British is correct, causes much needless offence to Scottish, Ulster and Welsh listeners. It is a common error but one which is easily avoided by proper care on the part of writers and producers. At the same time we should not hesitate to use the word 'English' if it is the proper description.' For some reason, it's quite rare for the Welsh or Northern Ireland audiences to react with anything like the ferocity of the Scots.

Great care and attention needs to be paid to the correct use of the Union Flag (not the Union Jack). It has been flown for winners representing England, although it is more correctly the 'British Flag' – not the 'English flag', thus doubly enraging many a non-English viewer. A victory for England should of course be marked with the flag of St George. But this can be confusing to host broadcasters who sometimes think that the Union flag 'will do'. To add insult to injury, the Union flag is all too often flown upside down.. 'Darn Me! They have done it again!', boomed one correspondent in a letter addressed to 'The BBC Commissioner': 'The correct way to fly the flag is in fact to have, at the flagstaff edge, the narrow white stripe at the foot of the flag. When flown with the broad stripe at the foot it is in fact a signal of distress! COME ON BBC, LEAD THE WAY!'

For many, many years prior to devolution, the duty office logs constantly reminded programme makers, heads of department and BBC management of these strands of offence. So the publication of New Labour's 'nationhood guidelines' signalled something of a blessed relief for those at the coalface of accountability. For it came to pass that BBC mandarins had to provide an official edict to the effect that extreme care was henceforth required in defining matters deemed to be 'English' or 'British'. So much so that mischievous reports began appearing in the tabloids claiming that the BBC was set on banning the use of 'British' and 'Nation'. This naturally led to a flood of complaints lambasting the BBC for 'again undermining the very fabric of this country'. 'Shame on you all', one caller echoed on behalf of a shocked nation south of Watford, 'and may God forgive you.'

The BBC has always been vulnerable on the wider xenophobic front. Such perceptions can arise from even the most peaceful of events. For example, the entente was less than cordiale during coverage of the opening ceremony of the Channel Tunnel. Here, many a continental cousin (able to receive BBC broadcasts) complained about an unhealthy dose of BBC chauvinism. They were deeply unimpressed to learn of this 'historic moment for the continent of Europe, which will no longer be separated from the British Isles.' Another of Mrs Thatcher's BBC grievances voiced during the Falklands War was the use of such terminology as 'The Government' and 'The British forces', as opposed to our government or our forces. Ironically however, it was during the wartime leadership of Mrs T's hero, Winston Churchill, that it became right and proper to disassociate the reporting medium from the elected government of the people and troops loyal to the crown.

It wasn't until 1999 that the BBC finally addressed that other gripe of the regionally challenged. Each year, a regular hard core of English Licence fee payers raged about the BBC's lackluster attitude towards St.George's Day. Or more specifically the complete lack of any reference to it. Ardent English nationalists bemoaned the 'constant televising of the St. Patrick's Day March from America'. The BBC defence spanned two arguments. Firstly that St. George was no longer the patron saint of England; that position having been vacant for many years. The second was that it was not the BBC's function to promote Saints' Days but to cover any festivities or celebrations that were organized in celebration of them. Because there were no events organized in celebration of St. George's Day, there was nothing to report. This reasoning was immediately undermined by the sharper tools in the box who claimed to have spotted a plethora of St. Patrick's Day celebrations on the News, or daffodils 'stuffed into the lapels of every TV presenter on St. David's Day.'

The *Sun* newspaper had made a point each year of stirring up nationalistic pride. One year it urged its readers to have a go at an unpatriotic BBC for failing to promote St. George's Day. It provided a coupon as part of its campaign. This was supposed to be cut out and sent directly to the Controller of BBC-1, urging him to supply what all *Sun* readers 'urgently demanded for their licence fee'. Possibly the paper was aware that less than a dozen were received, which might have accounted for its stony silence thereafter.

Come 1999, instead of allowing the *Sun* to whip up its annual dissent among disenfranchised England's Saint Day enthusiasts, Auntie was for the first time ready with some pre-emptive strikes. These comprised a whole series of programmes specifically to do with, or closely associated with England's day. One in particular was featured in the *Counterblast* strand. This was a public access programme that provided a platform for views otherwise largely ignored by broadcasters. This particular edition featured a personal view of what it meant to be English.

Naturally there was a good deal of adverse pre-publicity. On the one hand there were allegations that the BBC was providing a platform for extreme right-wing propaganda. For anything attaching 'English' or 'Englishness' is instantly condemned as either racist or xenophobic. Conversely there were complaints that the BBC had heavy-handedly censored the film. At the end of the day a man stood in front of the camera and explained what it meant to him to be English. No apology. No qualification. He was proud to be an Englishman and said so. Despite all the pre-transmission tabloid bluster well over 100 viewers called to register their appreciation.

• Lobby Groups

The official BBC line when it comes to dealing with organised lobby groups is not to recongise them. In this, the worst thing that promoters of opinion can do is to make it known what they are doing. Far more powerful is the spontaneity factor, or even the single voice proffering such an elemental degree of basic good sense that it cannot be ignored. More than most, *Blue Peter* used to have its fair share of disclaimers during live transmission. The drying of the Blue Peter dog with an electric hair dryer when the animal was soaking wet is one example.

When *Dallas*, one of the best-loved soaps of all time, was dropped from the schedules, such was the spontaneous reaction from so many fans that it was reinstated. Unlike the demise of Radio's *Listen With Mother* and Television's *Blake's Seven* back in the 1970s. These either became issues of 'national concern' according to the tabloids, or the domain of blatant lobby groups. Hundreds of letters were once received following press reports that Humanists would be allowed to contribute to Radio 4's *Thought for the Day*. Arguments made by listeners for and against the notion was split 50-50, with both sides begging the BBC not to take any notice of the opposing view. Christian listeners wrote to the Head of Religious Broadcasting, while the Humanists wrote to the Director-General. 'The organisation behind a pile of almost identical letters is very easy to spot,' wrote one former Head of Programme Correspondence. 'Multiple, borrowed or fashionable opinion is no match for the heart-felt spontaneous point of view.'

Over 3,000 calls of complaint were received from demonstrators against the concept of the BBC's annual *Children In Need* Appeal. 'The Campaign Against Patronage' comprised groups representing people with disabilities. These groups were invited to demonstrate outside Television Centre and to have 'Fun with Fones'. The plan was to immobilise BBC switchboards by calling in 'for the hell of it to tell them how you feel,' and to 'make the bastards squirm!' Fans of the cult Sci-Fi series *Dr Who* were not slow in spotting the potential of this tactic. Here was yet another opportunity to try to force the BBC into reinstating the series.

In fairness, the plan was really quite ingenious. It called for around 25,000 fans from around the world to each make 20 calls to Television Centre on a given day. This, according to the protest co-ordinator, would represent around half a million phone calls, which the BBC could hardly ignore. Unfortunately, as with the *Children In Need* lobby, the plan was stymied by the very fact that such organised lobbies are rarely publicity shy. Special arrangements were put in place to ensure that other business of the BBC did not suffer. Despite the 'global strength of feeling' promoted by the organizer, less than a thousand 'Whovians' bothered to call.

In 1991 *The Independent* newspaper called on its readers to 'jam the BBC switchboards.' This was in demand of a new series of the cult classic: *Twin Peaks*. Possibly saying a lot more about the *Independent*'s readership or the feckless fans of the series, few calls were received. Then there was the group of individuals who had learned of a repeat screening of Michael Palin's epic trek *Around the World in 80 Days*. One of the programmes in the series contained graphic pictures of a snake being skinned and gutted alive. Incredibly this had somehow escaped the nation's attention the first time round. The most appalling images of things happening to human beings can fill the screen without so much as a whimper. But showing cruelty to an animal in any form guarantees a huge reaction. However, despite all the press attention, the re-screening of the hapless snake's unfortunate end resulted in just two complaints.

In 1992 the nation was blessed with the arrival of BBC Television's latest offering on the soap front, *El Dorado*. More than enough has already been written about this saddest of episodes in the annals of BBC Television drama, not to dwell on the subject here. Suffice to say that throughout and following its first episode it continued to attract hundreds of complaints and the unfailing attention of the tabloids and media pundits alike. It was condemned out of hand as 'pure, unadulterated rubbish'. Its life span was a short and bitter one. The nation, the press, focus groups and even politicians had spoken, and the BBC listened. Yet, no sooner had the screen been cleared of this object of derision than there appeared a new lobby group determined to pressure the BBC into reversing its decision.

154

A coach party even appeared at the gates of Television Centre crowded with supporters. Viewer & Listener Correspondence received some 6,500 supporters coupons clipped from *TV Times*. Close on 3,000 letters and 11 box files from TEASE (The Eldorado Appreciation Society Espana) also arrived. Incredibly, a large number of these lobbyists admitted that they were amongst the thousands that stridently urged the BBC not to continue wasting their licence fee 'on such utter rubbish.' Now they were pleading for the series to return. A similar fate befell another lackluster TV series. Set in the world of racehorse training, *Trainer*, as it was imaginatively entitled, had survived two seasons and was teetering on the edge of indecision for a third. Slated generally throughout its run, fans fearful of its demise began a similar campaign.

On the radio at the same time, 'another victory for the chattering classes', was the clarion call following the demise of Radio 4's *Anderson Country*. Since this programme began it had attracted mountains of letters and stacks of calls demanding it and its presenter, Gerry Anderson (no, not he of *Thunderbirds* fame), to be 'removed from the Radio 4 schedule.' However, no sooner had the deed been done than just as many 'fans' began writing and telephoning to complain. A report written at this time suggested that 'favourably disposed viewers and listeners tend generally to contact the BBC only when they fear a show will be axed'. It suggested that there is just as much value in letting broadcasters know when programmes are appreciated as when they are not. In the case of *Trainer* particularly, it was just another horse that had already bolted.

One lobby group attached a film that was never actually screened. Over a ten-week period, 500 calls and twice as many letters were received from churchgoers all over the country. They had been led to believe that the *The Last Temptation of Christ* was planned as the big Easter film. This was of course not the case. But the facts did little placate the incredible strength of feeling aroused by such a good story. The BBC had indeed bought the rights to show the film but never did. That was left to Channel 4 who showed it a few years later to a huge wave of indifference. It did however leave the BBC with the legend of Wendy Hardtop.

Towards the end of this lengthy and bitter campaign many a call and letter was being registered or addressed for the attention of Wendy Hardtop, of whom no one had ever heard. And herein lies a lesson for all would-be lobby coordinators. A supporter in Bradford (for example) would stretch an already extensive Chinese whisper to a friend in Bournemouth (for example), who would then (for example) pass on the word to a colleague in York. In so doing, crucial details such as names can become corrupted.

One day a lobbyist was asked (politely) to explain exactly who was this Wendy Hardtop. The enquiry was greeted with much incredulity: "You mean you don't even know your own Controller of BBC-1?" Then it became clear. In the course of this exceptionally extensive whisper, the real name of the Controller of BBC-1 had become corrupted. Wendy Hardtop had in fact replaced Alan Yentob.

• Sex, Violence, Taste & Decency

Incidents of Sex and Violence are not to be confused with Taste and Decency. The difference between these BBC categories should be straightforward but it is not. This is possibly because tradition dictates that the two sit together even though they do not automatically go together. Mary Whitehouse might well have been responsible for the confusion. Her clean-up TV campaign highlighted that 'too much sex & violence in our living rooms' was in poor taste and an affront to decency.

In actual fact, very few people complain about the amount of sex and violence on television. Indeed the proverbial 'Disgusted from Tonbridge Wells is more likely to ask where it is. To put the matter into perspective, *Points of View* viewers did not react to news of a Broadcasting Standards Council set up to keep the BBC and other broadcasters in check. Instead, close on one hundred of them wrote to complain about presenter Anne Robinson's new haircut.

So what does Taste and Decency mean? The infamous peeing competition featured in the children's series *Round the Twist* falls into this category. It was enjoying its third outing, and was attracting the same complaints from disgusted parents (although the kids themselves loved it). So why continue to enrage viewers by retaining a known offending scene? The answer is because the peeing competition was integral to the plot. It's what (some) little boys like to do. It's not to everyone's taste, and there we have it.

Taste & Decency is a very 'BBC' type category; one that covers a multitude of otherwise unfathomable comment, complaint and criticism. From the outset, 'the Official Organ of the BBC' (*Radio Times*), was seen not only as an important source of programme information, but also as the arbiter of public Taste.

A letter published in the very first edition (28 September 1923) asked: 'Do they really think that the majority of listeners are really interested in such lectures as the Decrease of Malaria in Great Britain, How to Become a Veterinary Surgeon – etc?'

'Why,' the pioneering pundit wanted to know, 'is it apparently not thought advisable to repeat *Request Nights*,' which he considered more popular than 'the steady stream of worthy classical programmes'. 'Frankly,' he expanded, 'it seems to me that the BBC are mainly catering for the tastes of "Listeners" who own expensive sets and pretend to appreciate and understand only highbrow music and education 'snob stuff'.' The BBC should operate 'like a theatre manager. They must put up programmes which will appeal to the majority - who provide the main bulk of their income'.

Seventy years later, a mother rang Television Centre to complain bitterly that the BBC did nothing to cater for her children's very particular tastes during the school holidays. On putting it to her that not every programme would be suited to everyone all of the time, came the response: "Bugger everyone else. What the hell am I expected to do with these kids all day?" 'Taste' therefore largely depends on an individual's own personal worldview. 'Bad Taste' is another matter. For example, a caller once demanded that a programme dubbed in Hindi be taken off his screen immediately as he considered it to be in bad taste.

As did the distraught mother who complained that the phrase 'prehistoric turd' was used in an episode of *Birds of a Feather*. Whereas 'putting a hedgehog down your knickers' was considered to be a lapse in decency. One mention of 'bog roll' and the lines become lively, for the correct term (especially in the Home Counties) is 'lavatory paper'.

The BBC has a responsibility to broadcast programmes within accepted boundaries of taste and decency that do not set out gratuitously to offend. Sometimes it gets it wrong. There was the TV producer who set out to achieve the same notoriety as did Orson Wells on American radio. It was he who infamously scared America half to death in the 1930s with his production of War of the Worlds. Some 60 years later, BBC Television's *Ghostwatch* was billed as an 'appropriate drama for Hallowe'en'. Except that over a thousand viewers on the night made it abundantly clear that they were 'confused', 'angry', 'sickened', 'bemused' and 'frightened'.

In all, over 2,000 viewers complained that they 'felt conned by a programme and broadcaster they thought they could trust'. Hundreds of others protested that it was 'irresponsible' and 'in the poorest possible taste'. There had been other Hallowe-en specials in the past that came and went without so much as a whimper. Except of course for the *Paul Daniels; Live at Hallowe-en* back in 1987. This had resulted in 800 calls on the night complaining of 'Satanism'; 'dabbling in the occult' and 'promoting evil'. The BBC made it clear then that it would never happen again.

A senior Light Entertainment producer once defended his right to 'walk the tightrope of taste' by dismissing the 200 viewers who had called in to complain about his programme. With viewing figures of some two million, he summarily dismissed the reaction as little more than 'two people asking for their money back at a Cup Final'. Back in the 1920s, John Reith identified those 'who seem incapable of tuning in expecting only to hear those programmes guaranteed not to be to their taste'. There was the 'respectable gentleman living in a respectable suburb of a respectable town' who forbad his daughters to listen to love songs or dance music. Reith feared such a person would never again 'look leniently on the BBC.'

Even though the 1920s might have been roaring away elsewhere, solid Edwardian principles strictly dictated what could and could not be broadcast by the BBC. So it is all the more delightful to imagine Reith - the strict, autocratic Scottish Presbyterian - lending himself to an unexpected degree of candour. A highly respectable woman entered her drawing-room only to hear wafting from her radio, the phrase: 'great tits like coconuts'. After switching the set off in disgust, she immediately set pen to paper to lay into the BBC for 'polluting the ether and debasing womanhood'. Nonplussed, Reith replied: 'Dear Madam, if you had only continued listening you would also have heard that robins like worms!'

Matters of Decency are more about behaviour. What is 'grossly offensive' to one sector of the audience is a joy to another. One 'small voice of irritation' drew attention to the manner in which actors in television plays were 'made to throw a discarded jacket or usually a raincoat over a peg instead of using the loops provided in the garment for hanging it properly'. Another complained about the cast of *EastEnders* drinking out of bottles instead of using glasses. This was seen as being somehow responsible for teenagers 'acting like tramps'. 'They don't have any training nowadays', the complainant thundered, 'parents sitting in pubs all day – if they have any parents at all!'

Another BBC complaint category 'English usage' can also fall under the Taste & Decency banner. Newsreaders, weather people, continuity announcers and 'other scientists of the spoken word' are thoroughly admonished whenever and however they might 'render the vowel sounds into the sewers and cesspits of slovenliness'. Immediately pounced upon is the poor pronunciation of words such as sound, round, loud or cloud that 'defile the ear' as 'sand, rand, lad and clad'. One irate Radio 4 listener suggested that a recording of 'claddy wevva from the saafwest emitted from the maaf of the weverman' should be

played to all BBC staff over loudspeakers each day as a reminder
of their responsibility to the English language.

Few would argue that if the English language is safe anywhere it
is within the rarified atmosphere or Radio 4. But even this
guardian of the spoken word like what it should be spoke is not
immune from attack. 'I am wondering', wrote one listener, 'just
how and where the BBC of today goes about getting its staff.
The Continuity Announcer (if that title can rightly be afforded
in this instance) said that 'next on Radio 4 would be *You and
Yours*. Then she added that it followed the news summary –
'so it CAN NOT be "next" can it?! The News was quite clearly
NEXT!'

Then there is the matter of 'foul language'. Reith recalled the Aunt who was almost sure she heard 'Botheration!' foul the airwaves during the Children's Hour. There are still those so shocked that they actually count the number of swear words in programmes. Indeed, within the BBC world there is kept a category of swear words by which to gauge likely audience reaction.

This list carries the full Monty of each and every offensive Anglo-Saxon contribution to the English language. Beginning at the very top with the 'C- word' derivative of Berkshire Hunt, down to the blasphemous 'bloody'. It can be very amusing to have a plumy BBC accent proffering advice and guidance on the subject, much as a good waiter does with the wine list. But even this level of care and attention offers no guarantee of success. A single feature film that contained no less than 159 uses of the 'F' word scored less on the Richter scale of complaints than when one of the characters in *The Archers* uttered the word 'piss'.

Ace cockney bigot, Alf Garnett, returned to the screen in the 90s much to the horror the fast emerging politically correct. Despite years of huge publicity and great public debate, the whole point of the character continued to be lost on those ready and willing to be shocked (invariably on behalf of *others*). For millions, Christmas wouldn't be Christmas without a decent helping of the comedy classic *Only Fools and Horses*. But even after so many years, there will always be one viewer 'shocked and startled' by the language used in it. Not that long ago, one disgruntled caller complained that 'one doesn't expect to endure such terminology as 'plonka' in one's lounge at this time of the year'.

Quite why sex shares the same bed as violence is a bit of a conundrum. It sort of implies the two go hand in hand, whereas sex, more than violence, is more easily confused with perceptions of taste or decency. Arguably, Violence is more straightforward. A decision was taken to end one series of the highly popular hospital drama *Casualty* with a bit of a bang. Or more correctly, an ultra-violent Armageddon of Hollywood disaster movie proportions. Set against the carefully nurtured realism of Holby General, the sheer lunatic departure of this otherwise excellent series sent the Television Information Office call counter into deep overdrive. Call after call after call after call came in from the angry and the bewildered screaming this was not what they expected from such a trusted family favourite. Cars were crashing into ambulances, people and patients were rioting or careering in flames down exploding lift shafts. Life at Holby General had suddenly and inexplicably and for no apparent reason morphed into a cross between *Die Hard* and *Apocalypse Now*.

A columnist from *The Daily Mail* once did time at the coalface of accountability. He arrived armed with a highly specific brief; to root out the truth surrounding 'public concern' about too much sex and violence on the small screen. His expectations were clear as to what he would witness following the second part of a particularly raunchy drama called *The Men's Room*.

167

This was a series that had enjoyed column yards in the tabloids for its on-the-knuckle, highly salacious sex scenes. An excellent choice therefore with which to witness the public's outrage and disgust as it was happening. At least, that was the great expectation. His day began with an investigation of the Correspondence Section and the two and half thousand letters it received every week. Of those, a mere nine complaints had been received about what the tabloids had considered 'the seamiest segment' in the first episode of *The Men's Room*. Sadly, there was not a jot else about sex and violence in the weeks either side of it. Only a letter from a woman who refused to have sex rammed down her throat.

In the evening the hunt was taken to the Television Duty Office, where reaction to the previous week's episode of *The Men's Room* was muted. A paltry three calls were logged. According to the tabloids that particular episode was what you might expect to see in a 'Hong Kong porno house.' One of the three callers had never been to a Hong Kong porno house and wanted to know if the rest of the series was going to be just as good. A tad embarrassing for the columnist whose paper had claimed the BBC switchboard was 'jammed all night' with angry viewers. By the time the end credits rolled, there hadn't been a single call of complaint. Not even during *the* scene - one of those interludes where you can only marvel at the imagination, dexterity (and sheer sexual stamina) of fellow human beings.

• Repeats

Once a *Sun* reader telephoned to voice his agreement with that paper's Leader condemning the number of repeats on BBC TV. He added in his support for the view that his favourite newspaper would not dream of repeating the same story in the same edition. Except on that day, the same *Sun* Spot appeared twice.

The press and opinion formers have for decades constantly carped on behalf of a nation 'deluged with repeats of old programmes'. Yet the repeating of programmes has never been a big issue with viewers and listeners themselves. Once, over 700 viewers rang to complain that the much-repeated – and very old - feature film *Easter Parade* had been re-scheduled in favour of sport coverage. With regard to repeats, the BBC continued to miss a trick. Even with just the four channels to choose from, it was never possible for viewers to watch every programme across all channels all of the time. Mind you, there was the one viewer who reckoned he sat in front of four TV sets and watched everything, morning noon and night. But there cannot have been that many sad individuals about.

The reality of the matter is that more viewers have requested more repeats than have complained about them. Particularly those that the tabloids had given a rave revue, or condemned as filthy or depraved. It took until the dawn of the New

169

Millennium for the BBC to realize that it had nothing to continually apologise for. That for every one complaint about 'being forced to suffer repeats', as many as 30 or 40 requests were received for them. Witness now those paying premium prices on top of the licence fee in order to watch endless streams of old BBC programmes on rival commercial channels. Bizarre, given the amount of stick given the BBC for the crime of repeating them free.

• **Change**

They say that the three core ingredients of conversation most likely to generate conflict, and therefore best avoided, are sport, politics and religion. Fortunately in Britain there are other topics aside from Beckham, Blair and God that drag trite conversation into the realms of absolute but safe banality. Top banana is The Weather followed closely by what was on television the previous night, and in particular the News. Vast numbers have 'watched The News' for so long that it has assumed something a life form of its own. And here expectations are infinite. One early listener complained: "Why do you only announce the deaths of great men? Why not also announce their births?"

Any change to the format of Television News will guarantee a storm of protest. Changes in recent years have been condemned as 'pseudo-American', complete with 'tacky, tawdry and distracting graphics'. In the mid-90s, what appeared to be twin forks of lightning clashed dramatically centre screen. Together with a Wagnerian-sounding musical sting, this was considered as 'neo-nazi in its concept'. Even use of the latest computer-generated effects has taken its toll. When the first 'virtual studios' came on line, dozens of viewers complained about the waste of having a solitary newsreader occupy such a vast space. Whereas in fact most lawn mowers enjoy more room in the garden shed.

Mostly the use of new technology is accepted and understood, but initially there was much to vex the technologically challenged. Take the massive-looking 'glass' cube that once incorporated the BBC crest heralding the start of BBC TV news. This computer generated feature appeared to be suspended from the (virtual) studio ceiling. The camera would pan down from it to zoom into the newsdesk. This was not only reckoned to be needlessly extravagant, but something of a genuine hazard. A BBC governor aired his Health & Safety concerns about the contrivance, fearing for the consequences should the huge and weighty looking object break loose and come crashing down onto the hapless newsreader below.

Great emphasis is placed on the BBC's unrivalled reputation for its News service. However, changes to News programming can generate more adverse comment than its complete removal. In 1975 there was the very first strike by BBC journalists. To say the least, the reaction from licence fee payers was surprising. They were in the main 'delighted'. Indeed some considered the loss of News to have been be 'the nicest thing that has happened for a long time'. Similar reaction has followed whenever industrial action has disrupted normal service. Alternative programming has invariably been perceived as 'much better instead of beastly news'. But some things are truly sacrosanct. There are two very clear set pieces whereby any notion of change in any form is not negotiable. Radio 4 is one and The Weather is the other.

Once, changes to both the style and the transmission timings of The Weather briefly came about as a result of a new-look Television News. This meant that viewers were 'forced' to sit through both the National and Regional programmes before kneeling at the altar of The Weather. Worse still was when the bulletin following the Nine O'clock News was 'savaged' by halving its airtime from two minutes to one. And horrors upon horror, the graphics were also changed. The nation went ape: 'changes do nothing but make the forecast meaningless to fishermen'….. 'Incomprehensible twaddle'… 'without any thought to the retention of wind direction'…'Mickey Mouse animation'…. 'The souring of a perfectly adequate service, punctuated by the demise of the Isobar!'… 'Rushed, confused'… 'Maps too small'… 'No overnight temperatures, vital to gardeners and animals'…. 'of no use to fishermen'…. 'sailors'…. 'shoppers'… 'fishermen'… 'caravaners' … 'walkers'… 'climbers'… 'fishermen'… 'glider pilots'… 'hot air balloonists'…(and) 'fishermen'.

The BBC lamely issued an excuse. The new graphics were designed to provide a simplified forecast to fit the reduced broadcast time. But such was the outrage it was conceded that the changes were 'perhaps not best favoured by most viewers and therefore would be better placed where tradition and expectation dictated'. In plain English this meant that the BBC had got it hopelessly wrong and that there would be a smart return to the old format, which there was.

So it was with no small amount of trepidation that greeted the decision to drop Fahrenheit in favour of Celsius. Here, serious internal concerns were expressed on behalf of the meteorologically challenged. How would they cope? Were we bowing to political pressure or being bullied by Brussels? No matter what the reason it was simply a matter of battening down the hatches and expecting the worst. The switchboard was primed. The Information Offices stood by to mop up the deluge of complaints following the first pro-Celsius forecast. Except that, despite an odds-on, sure-fire bet of a barrage, no one noticed. Celsius crept into the nations psyche to a thunderous whimper of indifference. There was however one vengeful licence payer determined to find the person responsible.

Having been passed from pillar to post, the lay but deeply enthusiastic meteorologist, settled into the ear of a member of BBC Television staff. It transpired that, according to the caller's calculations, 765 billion raindrops had fallen over the UK during the autumn period. He being an 'Imperial man' wanted to know therefore how he was expected to arrive at a comparator from gallons to calculate the specific density of cubic metres? There are moments when the running of a length of coarse sandpaper across the eyeball can be a more pleasurable experience than picking up the telephone.

When it comes to changes to longstanding favourites on BBC radio, a person has to either be foolhardy or brave, or both. For close on 30 years, Radio 1 was the only national popular music channel. Radio 2 occupied the middle of the road music slot and Radio 3 the classical. Radio 4 was the 'speech' channel. Radio 5 was originally designed to carry education, youth and sport programmes with a selection of World Service output. But as time has moved on it chiefly caters for News and Sport. Once established, commercial channels would provide fierce competition. Radio 1 was for too long perceived as none too cool in the eyes of its target audience. And Talk Radio was already making inroads into Radio 4 territory.

The splitting of Radio 4 into Radio 4 FM and Radio 4 Long Wave proved highly controversial. Shifting *Yesterday in Parliament* from its regular slot after the indomitable *Today* programme aggrieved politicians especially. They, together with thousands of other ordinary mortals, saw no merit in 'demoting'

Yesterday in Parliament to the 'Siberian wastelands of Long Wave'. The *Morning Service* was also shifted out of mainstream Radio 4 after close on seventy years. A listener from Watford had the idea for a daily religious service in 1928, which had remained part of the daily schedule ever since.

The ousting of *Woman's Hour* from its traditional afternoon slot to mid-morning was also deeply unpopular. Hundreds of faithful listeners felt the programme was fine where it was. It wasn't broke and didn't need fixing. Generations, it was argued, had grown accustomed to its place in the daily routine on the home front. But it was this very picture of 'the little woman' at home doing 'womanly things' that did not compute with the thrusting 90s lifestyle. Research indicated that there was now a new, more diverse audience out there; one 'more deserving to be served'. It was archaic, dated, and anachronistic to think otherwise. Besides, an earlier slot for *Woman's Hour* would suit 'the overall business' more effectively, if not all its customers.

Radio 2 listeners were fired into action about the changes to their favourite channel. A primary target was new cardigan on the block, John Sachs. He managed to upset hundreds of listeners by playing 'the kind of music not usually associated with Radio 2'. Despite 600 complaints bemoaning the decision to do so, firm favourites Benny Green and Allan Dell were both given their marching orders. The commercial station

Classic FM was now on the national scene. It was posing a real threat to the 'purity' of Radio 3's unadulterated, hardcore classical output. Attempts to make it more populist in the face of commercial competition spelt a diminution of traditional quality. Despite a very public outrage, many a stalwart Radio 3 presenter enjoyed their last night at the proms, including Richard Baker. Many mourned his departure and mercilessly berated his successors.

Changes of format can either be upsetting or long overdue. The venerable *Question Time* became the focus of much criticism when it (briefly) changed its style of presentation. Fans of the programme were appalled to witness the morphing of David Dimbleby into something 'more akin to a quiz show host'. He would invite each eminent panelist 'to come on down' or more shockingly "remove himself from the chair' before striding down into the audience to seek out the questioners. Happily, his habit of 'constantly and rudely interrupting audience and guests alike' remained to offer a little stability in an ever-changing BBC world.

For years, those commentating on the London Marathon commentated too much. The cameras always got in the way and 'excessive coverage was afforded the front runners' to the detriment of 'women, juniors, disabled and fun runners'. Commentary and cameras aside, the latter was deemed to be unfair and 'against the whole spirit of the event.' Complaints poured in each year that the BBC ignored those who had spent months training hard for their big day. And what of those giving to charity being denied seeing their sponsored novelty runner in action? When the 'listening BBC' finally responded, many considered the changes to be patronizing. The BBC was accused of 'ghettoising' the disabled and those dressed as carrots, rhinos or portable toilets.

• Information

If you think that Information does not constitute a category for complaint or controversy, then think again. There was the professional wood turner who wanted to know what the space was between the spindles of a staircase featured on *EastEnders*. It was confirmed that they were set more than 90mm apart. This constituted a serious contravention of building regulations, and in turn a breach of Health and Safety. Then there was the other *EastEnders* viewer. He rang to make an offer on one of the vehicles on sale in the used car lot. When the switchboard operator told him that they were props and not actually for sale, he demanded to be put through to the duty officer to complain that the BBC was guilty of "stifling free enterprise".

When it comes to information provision, few other organizations can compare with the sheer size and diversity of the BBC. Here, not even the finest information technology can guarantee 100% customer satisfaction. Take the request for full details of 'the electromagnetism theory of time and symmetry'. Apparently, this was featured in a BBC television (or radio) programme 'about 20 years ago'. Or 'official BBC accreditation' that the raccoon is not the only animal to have a bone in its penis. The walrus is likewise blessed (in fact it has a much larger one, known as an oosik). Whereas a zoo is better placed to answer that, what about confirmation that a set of Siamese twins

179

was once spontaneously separated after listening to the 1812 overture on the radio?

Before the advent of Daytime Television, the BBC used to fill the screen with the picture of a little girl holding a doll. A curious assembly of lines, shapes and numbers, which allowed TV engineers and retailers to tune-in television sets, framed her. The music played as a backing to this service in turn created hoards of enquiries for details of what each track was, and where it could obtained. Unfortunately none of it was commercially available as it was all non-copyright. Of course this offered no discouragement to hundreds of callers who were happy to obtain just the title and the composer.

Now this might sound straightforward enough, but because it was all non-copyright, any track from a multiple of discs could be played at anytime according to what was to hand. Because no forms had to be filled in there was no record kept of what was played nor when. The whole thing was more a matter of chance. It has to be said that there were some very nice pieces played and seasoned staff could recite the details of the most popular in their sleep. And often did. This particularly battered old file was duly dispatched to the BBC's Written Archive Centre at Caversham in the sure and certain knowledge that one day, someone, somewhere would be salivating over its contents. Sure enough, there exists today a Trade Transmissions Test Card Appreciation Society.

For most programmes over many years, the supply of information for members of the public was not a priority. Many were excellent at sending out copies of post-production paperwork containing heaps of information from music to location details and so on. But beyond that, programme makers understandably had programmes to get out on air and could not always spare the time to hunt down extra information. Once, the two most feared production areas to call on behalf of a member of the public were News and Sport. Unless you had the ability to sound just as stressed-out, harassed and pissed-off as they, and could condense a request for help into a four second sound bite then you didn't stand a chance. For others it was not so much the rudeness or the discourtesy as much as the sheer indifference. For example, one weekday afternoon a very familiar voice came through to the Television Duty Office wanting to get hold of some material from BBC Sport.

It took only a few rounds of cautious questioning to establish absolutely the caller's identity. Nevertheless, it always pays to double check, so the hotel was called back and their illustrious guest confirmed. Then began the awesome tasks of trying to (a) get an answer from the Sports Department (b) get someone to listen, (c) convince them that it was a genuine call and (d) hope they'd do something. Even then, Sport's tenuous affinity with the notion of customer care was likely to evaporate between (b) and (c) along with any notion of basic civility. Such was the pressure on their every waking minute that invariably calls to them would be answered with a loud and fevered demand to know "WHAT????!!!!" There was no choice in these situations but to plough on; it had to be understood that this was their way.

In this instance it took just a few dozen calls to a small army of deeply unimpressed Sports personnel with obviously far better things to do with their time. Eventually the Contracts Manager for BBC Sport turned out to be less indifferent than his colleagues and was persuaded to at least call the hotel. After all, the only alternative was for someone else to explain why the BBC generally and who in particular was not prepared to help. An hour or so later the sporting legend was back on the line simply to say: "Thanks". This was followed by another call from the Contracts Manager who was going to deliver the material personally. After all, he gushed, it's not every day you get the chance to meet Muhammed Ali.

What the BBC pumps out by the hour across an ever-increasing range of services is as diverse as it is mind-boggling. By the time it takes you to finish reading this paragraph, someone somewhere will be wanting to know more about national literacy, global pollution, the Heritage Seed Programme, Bullyline or the plight of black bears in China. Or things medical such as cerebella ataxia, Alzheimer disease, cranio-synostosis, asthma, Desert Storm Sickness, facial Palsy, Manoplax, rosacea and Hurler's Syndrome. And anything associated with cancer, back pain, religious cult activity and hair loss.

Together with the more technically vexing, Engineering Information (now Reception Advice) can plough its way through endless enquiries as to what radio or video recorder to buy; which make has what new gadget and would Uncle Albert (who's 95) be able to work it? And all the while, with some fresh horror lurking in some dark corner somewhere out there.

A man once complained that a neighbour was controlling his television set. After much investigation by BBC Engineers the true culprit was revealed. The complainant had recently fitted a low energy light bulb. These apparently emit energy across the entire light spectrum, including the infra-red band used to control TV sets and the like. This then led to the random selection of channels each time he switched on the light. The lamp manufacturers' solution was to place a bunch of flowers in front of the television.

Writers, researchers, students and academics tend to look upon the BBC as something of a free and easy research facility. Of course they are assisted wherever possible and when it is

reasonable to do so, but sometimes however, the expectations are less than realistic. One young lady for example was working on an 8000 word dissertation for her national diploma on fashion. Comparing the lifestyles of the first and last Chinese emperors was the theme; an area the BBC must have covered fully in its time. Her list of requirements included samples of material, postcards, posters, booklets, photos, leaflets, photocopies and appropriate video material. She kindly advised "not to rush, but to take your time" in order to "collect the information properly." A French student of ethnology wanted a complete run down of "all the films, ancient and recent" which featured 'natural people' anywhere in the world, adding, thoughtfully, just "a catalogue or a descriptive list" would suffice.

Then there are those moments when credibility can be pushed to the limit. A caller wanted to know how she could get in touch with the late celebrity medium, Doris Stokes. Unfazed by this, the Assistant handling the call proffered the number of the National Spiritualist Association. This information had found its way onto the information database following a call taken just after the death of actress Dame Peggy Ashcroft. Here, the caller claimed to have just been speaking to her, to which the Assistant taking the call replied, in all innocence, "but she's dead." " I know that," spat the caller, "I'm a medium. Dame Peggy just wanted me to let you know how much she is looking forward to watching her tribute programme this evening."

Probably the all-time classic information request came in the form of the old lady and her enquiry regarding nuclear bunkers. It was in the early eighties that the BBC finally decided to show the banned documentary film *War Games*, which was until then thought to be so awesome that it could never be screened. Some 20 years after it was made, the (then) ever-inventive Controller of BBC-2 decided to schedule a week of nuclear holocaust programmes, of which *War Games* was to be one. Grim though it was, it hardly measured up to the devastating effects on the public that the BBC governors had in their wisdom once feared it would. It did however serve to liven up things in the Television Duty Office as large numbers of people began ringing in for details of how they could obtain a nuclear bunker. Naturally, the office had pre-empted such requests and had to hand several brochures and manufacturers' addresses.

One caller was a sweet old lady who had decided to invest her life savings in a bunker of her very own. She was afforded patient assistance and off she went. Soon she was becoming something of a regular; seeking advice on storing food, air circulation and how best to deal with her solid waste. She was a dear old soul and this was the BBC. Eventually, after several weeks had passed, no more was heard from her. Until one day she rang again, armed with her near-complete list. The news was good: a purchase was imminent. The site had been identified; the

style and composition of the structure had been decided upon;
life support systems had been selected and the decision to install
a CB radio resolved. Then came the matter of the door.

"Do you know," she asked, "if they do one with a cat-flap?"

LAST OF THE SUMMER WINE

The last in the long line of moves for Viewer & Listener Correspondence and Engineering Information came in August 1998 when they were decanted into the new Customer Service operations base at Television Centre. Engineering Information immediately adopted its new name of Reception Advice along with a workforce no longer comprising BBC Engineers but Technical Experts. Supported by a squad of Technical Assistants, the emphasis was now on serving the digitally daunted expected to swell the traditional customer base once the new technology was rolled out. VLC remained very much VLC with its largely unhappy few continuing to do what it had always done. Information Office staff remained in situ at Broadcasting House and Television Centre. The mixed economy of this disparate grouping made a mockery of the statistics necessary to measure the performance of the new service provider.

For the most part, a mixture of fatigue and demotivation resulted in a large proportion of the old guard more interested in redundancy than re-engineering. Despite an air of de-mob

189

happiness, the atmosphere remained civilised as everyone grappled to get their heads around a very surreal situation. Teams of prospective service providers asked the same questions and scribbled the same copious notes as the mysteries of the coalface unfolded. *The Times* spoiled the surprise for those of its readers who might feel 'obliged to pick up the telephone and tell the BBC just how delighted, or outraged, they are by Auntie's output'. They were informed that soon they would 'detect that the duty officers on the end of the line have assumed a new accent', as the BBC was shortly to 'award the privilege of dealing with such calls to a Call Centre in Belfast.'

The Radio Information Office closed in the February. Moved the previous year to accommodation of safe deposit proportions on the fourth floor at Broadcasting House, only a scribbled note hung from the door to mark this quiet moment in BBC history. March 31 saw the last letter go out from the Correspondence Section, exactly 75 years to the day since it pioneered the process. That same night the Television Information Office closed, silencing BBC telephones for the first time in sixty years. On All Fools Day 1999, the new BBC Information Centre in Belfast opened for business. For Capita agents and managers, realities of life at the coalface kicked in with a vengeance.

The bomb outrage in Omagh filled the screens for days with graphic images of this appalling act. When half the City of London was blown sky-high by a terrorist bomb, the sci-fi series *BUGS* was removed from the schedule as it contained a bomb-making sequence. But this didn't deter some fans from complaining. The BBC defended itself by drawing on its sensitivity to the situation. Except that later that same evening the comedy series *Harry Enfield and Chums* went out as planned together with a spoof sketch involving a bout of belligerent banter between Ian Paisley and Gerry Adams.

There was one near-miss on the information provision front. An email had come in wanting to know the name of David Frost's agent. A cursory check on the reply prior to its dispatch found nothing wrong with the tone of the reply. It politely thanked the enquirer for contacting the BBC and reported much happiness in being able to provide the required information. Except that it had down the agency as 'No Gay Artists' instead of Noel Gay Artists.

The nation reacted to the murder of television presenter, Jill Dando, as if it was the death of a close friend. A few pundits alluded to a similarity between Jill Dando's death and that of Diana, Princess of Wales. Death threats were made to prominent BBC figures so all otherwise loopy letters or telephone calls were afforded particular scrutiny. As the misery intensified in Kosovo and beyond, more death was delivered on the streets of London by way of a mystery nail bomber targeting minority groups. The dreaded Millennium Bug passed through the systems without a whimper, as did the BBC's complaints department into obscurity.

Just two days after the events of September 11th 2001, a questionable live edition of *Question Time* led to over 2,000 complaints of anti-US sentiment expressed by an audience 'full to bursting' with 'lefties', 'liberals' and 'terrorist sympathisers.' Close on the heels of Greg (Dyke)'s much publicised public apology for this, at least one broadsheet was demanding that Kate Adie be issued her P45 for tipping off the enemy about Tony Blair's secret trip to Oman. After another apology, this time directly to Number 10, it was found not to have been Ms Adie's fault. But no matter, tabloid and reader alike duly slammed into a 'treacherous BBC'. On the brighter side, new touch screen technology replaced Peter Snow's Gulf War sandpit. Instead of placing by hand plastic kit tanks and other machines of war, just the touch of a finger can now position 3-D submarines, ships and planes in just the right places.

The *Daily Mail* slated the BBC for its 'NEW SNUB TO QUEEN MOTHER'. Taken from comments made by the BBC-1 Controller that 'times have changed', decisions as to coverage in the event of the Queen Mother's death (or QMD as it is known in the trade) will now be made 'on the day'. The original instructions grimly and precisely laid out the plans for such an eventuality in meticulous detail. Solemn music would play across the national radio networks, heralding a nine-day period of official mourning. All programmes were required to be meticulously scoured for any untoward or indelicate reference to or about the deceased. Mawkish though it might appear, rehearsals regularly take place for the death of royals and major world leaders.

This obviously has to be done, but it can carry a price. Many hearts once stopped at Television Centre in the early 90s when Ceefax, the BBC's on-screen text service, reported live on air the death of the Queen Mother. Accounts vary from the report originating from Australia to a rehearsal at Television Centre that went horribly wrong. Mercifully, the broadcast lasted less than 40 seconds before it was spotted and largely went unnoticed by the public. But enough said about that as it not BBC policy to discuss such things. Suffice to say that the suggestion to "reduce the weight of importance of any future coverage is simply untrue".

So the process continues. And so it will for as long as there is a BBC. Meanwhile, there is absolutely nothing that can happen, at home or abroad, that will not have a tangible effect on those toiling at Auntie's coalface of accountability. They are never off duty. They cannot watch television, listen to the radio or read a newspaper without thinking what impact events at home and abroad are going to have on their working day.

Whatever is done, said by whom about what, or what decisions are taken from above, those at the coalface must be ready and waiting to mop up the mess. For as long as she exists, Auntie's adventures in the complaints trade will continue.

Bibliography

BBC
Written Archives
Host & Hostess 1925 – 1933 background material: Duties of the Duty Officer, June 1940; Control Board Minutes 1940
'Auntie BBC': reference to origins of term (from Economist 3.4.1954. p726)
17 April 1999: Capita: BBC Information Officially Opens

Ariel.
October 1964: Ronald Vivian: Duty Office
May 1974: Claudia Toler. 'Dear Sir….Now we are 50'.
13 August 1986: Cathy Loughran: 'All in the line of Duty'.
27 July 1988: Ed Harris: One to one with the world.
16 November 1988: Bill Hicks: New role of duty offices.
April / May 1998: Letters Page (EIEIO abbreviations correspondence)
September 29 1998. p3. Contract awarded for one-stop information center in Belfast.

Corporate
BBC Variety Programmes Policy Guide: For Writers and Producers. 1948
BBC Information Division. BBC Press Service. January 1988
Inside BBC Information: Reorganisation of Information Services. 16.9.88.
Courtesy & Care: A BBC Network Television guide to Relations with the Public. 1993.
BBC Handbook *1928 edition: Listeners' criticisms.*

The Listener
23 and 30 December 1982. Dave Rimmer: 'Good Evening Duty Office….'
23 April 1987.Langham Diary. Robert M Worcester.

Newspapers and Periodicals
The Independent on Sunday
4 July 1993. Lynn Barber. Independent on Sunday.
19 June 1994. Nick Cohen. Real Life: Ear-bashing Auntie. Independent on Sunday..
7 November 1999. Jane Robins. The Independent.

Daily Express
6 March 1963.Sally Cline: 'When they Bombard the BBC'.
3 February 1982. John Rydon and James Murray: Not so much a light comedy show….

Evening Standard

26 April 1994. The Alison Pearson column: A biting indictment of arrogant Auntie.
11 October 1991: David Shaw: One last push for Victory pleads Patten.
2 March 1994. Media: Christopher Morris: Bad-mouth the barking viewers.

Radio Times

Feb 17 1939.Harold Rathbone: The BBC Will Tell You: Telephone Enquiry Bureau:
June 26-July 2 1982. Bob Smyth. 'The BBC's Mailbag'.
1 February 1957. p.3. Sam Pollock: 'The BBC's Information Desk'.

Daily Mail

23 October 1986. p.19. Geoff Sutton and Patrick Hill: The Hotline of Shame; What viewers really think of BBC TV.
22 October 1991. John Edwards. The Way It Is: No room for complaint.

The Daily Telegraph

20 June 1992. Inside Track: Tabloid soap on the costa del sex 'n' sun.
18 February 1994. Max Davidson: When bog rolls and hedgehogs offend.

Time Out

9-16 June 1993. Time In: Aerial views. Elaine Paterson on duty officers.

Private Eye

January 1999: TV Eye: contracting out central complaints service.

The Times

5 June 1998. John Plunkett Interview with Brian Barwick: My Great Escape
13 January 1995 . p14. Libby Purves: How rude is the use of rude words?
25 July 1998. p25. Auntie looks ahead.:

PR Week

11-17 August 1988. Denis Budge: Watch with Auntie.

Radio Pictorial

29 November 1935. p10. 'Another "Behind the Scenes" Article by Whitaker-Wilson': The B.B.C Opens its letters.

TV Mirror

29 January 1955. Christopher Gould: 'Hullo is that lime Grove?' Interview with the Chief Television Liaison Officer.

Annabel Magazine

1986. *Kenric Hickson. Annabel Magazine: Dear Auntie....*

TV Guide

15 April 1989. Sue Platt. p45. I'm writing to complain.

Books

A social History of British Broadcasting Vol.One 1922-39. P Scannell. Blackwell 1991.
A Seamless Robe. C. Curran. Collins 1978
Action Stations! A History of Broadcasting House. Colin Reid. Robson Books.1987
Broadcast Over Britain. J.C.W. Reith. Hodder and Stoughton. 1924
Beyond the BBC. Tim Madge. Macmillan.1989
The BBC; The First Fifty Years. Asa Briggs. OUP.1985
The History of Broadcasting in the United Kingdom. Vols I & II. Asa Briggs. OUP. 1961/5
In and Out of the Box: Robert Dougall. HarperCollins.1973.
The Last Days of the Beeb. M Leapman. Allen and Unwin. 1986
Kill The Messenger. B Ignham. Fontana. 1991
The B.B.C And Its Audience. B S Maine. Nelson. 1939
The BBC: 70 years of Broadcasting. John Cain. BBC Books.1992
The Wireless Stars. George Nobbs. Wensum Books. 1972
Split Screen. Ian Trethowan. Hamish Hamilton. 1984
The Power Behind The Microphone. P P Eckersley. Cape. 1941
D G:The Memoirs of a British Broadcaster. A Milne. Hodder 1988.
BBC Engineering 1922-72. E. Pawlley. BBC 1972
The Network Tevelision Story. N. Moss. BBC. 1991
The Biggest Aspidistra in the World: A personal celebration of fifty years of the BBC. P. Black. BBC. 1972
What shall we do about the BBC? S. Milligan. Tory Reform Group. 1991
Here's Looking at You. The Story of British Television 1908-80.
Facing the Nation: Television and Politics 1936-76. G W Goldie. The Bodley Head. 1977

Fuzzy Monsters: Fear and Loathing at the BBC. Chris Horrie & Steve Clarke. Heinemann. *1994*

Chance Governs All by Marmaduke Hussey (Macmillan) 2001